Michael Parkinson is football daft. He caught the disease
from his father who stood for forty years in the same spot
watching Barnsley F.C., a remarkable feat of endurance
hitherto unrecorded. Michael Parkinson stood alongside his
father for sixteen of those years before leaving Barnsley to seek
his fortune elsewhere.

Since that time he has seen football in many countries
and once met a Laplander looking after a herd of reindeer
in the Arctic Circle who knew Danny Blanchflower.

When he is not writing about sport for the *Sunday Times*,
he is appearing on television or sitting at home watching for
signs of football mania in his three sons. Last year his vigilance
was rewarded when, on asking his five-year-old boy who he
most wanted to be when he grew up, he was told 'Bobby
Charcoal'.

His football heroes are Skinner Normanton (whom few
will know and whom God preserve), George Best, Bobby
Charlton and Freda Bucket who kissed him in the goalmouth
during a Ladies *v* Gents game in Yorkshire.

His favourite day is Saturday.

His favourite team is Manchester United.

His favourite colour is red (with white shorts).

He is not very old but looks much older and in
addition to the *Sunday Times* has written for the *Guardian*,
the *Observer*, *Punch*, the *Jerusalem Post* and the *Barnsley
Chronicle*.

Also in Arrow Books by Michael Parkinson

CRICKET MAD

Michael Parkinson

FOOTBALL DAFT

Cartoons by Graham

Arrow Books

Arrow Books Limited
3 Fitzroy Square, London W1

An imprint of the Hutchinson Group

London Melbourne Sydney Auckland
Wellington Johannesburg Cape Town
and agencies throughout the world

First published by Stanley Paul & Co. Ltd 1968
Published in Arrow Books 1973
© Michael Parkinson 1968

Made and printed in Great Britain by
Hunt Barnard Printing Ltd., Aylesbury, Bucks.

ISBN 0 09 908150 4

To anyone who is football daft

Contents

THE GAME'S THE THING

THE MAN IN THE MIDDLE

SEX AND SPORT

Acknowledgements

Some of the articles in this book were originally published in the *Sunday Times*. A number of the cartoons by Graham have already appeared in *Punch*.

I was five years old when I was taken to my first game of football. My father reminds me occasionally that at half time when he asked me how I liked it I said, 'It's all right but I think we'll go now'. To which he replied, 'I don't think we will', thereby making a decision which condemned me to a lifetime of addiction to the game. Out of that first tentative encounter grew a love affair which has lasted until the present without showing the slightest sign of weakening. The name of the lady is Barnsley and through the years—the few good ones, the many lean ones —I have loved her like my favourite blowzy barmaid. Even now it's easy to switch my mind back twenty years to the days when we caught the bus and made the five-mile journey into Barnsley to see the Reds play. The bus was always crowded with men in hairy overcoats and flat caps, smelling of Woodbines and last night's beer. At the station we would join the chattering throng as it surged up the hill and down the dip into the ground. Oakwell, the home of Barnsley Football Club, could not by any stretch of the imagination be called a pleasant spot, but no sight has thrilled me more, before or since, than the sudden view of the ground as we breasted the hill from the bus station and our eyes met the place where our heroes lived. Even now their names are easily remembered, like some familiar prayer: Binns, Harston, Shotton; Logan, Birkenshaw, Asquith; Smith, Cooling, Robledo, Barlow and McGarry. Inside the ground we would head for our favourite spot, to the east of the players' entrance on the terrace. It had been my father's spot for the past ten years, ever since he got a rise at the pit which enabled him to move from the back of the goals.

There we would be joined, week in week out, by our little but noisy family of regulars. There was the Maniac, charmingly called because of his towering outbursts of rage which occurred every time the opposition committed a foul. And Wobblygob, a spotty youth who earned his name through a pair of fulsome lips. This unfortunate act of nature was remarked most cruelly one Saturday by a Rotherham fan, who, tiring of the abuse being heaped on his team, turned round and said, 'Tha' could ride a bike round thi' gob'.

Together we shared the infinite pleasures and black despair which any football fan goes through following the fortunes of his team. It was in that same spot, with the view of the muck stacks on the other side, that I stood for fifteen years and saw many things both beautiful and ugly, sad and comic, and every Saturday grew more in love with the game. It was here that I first saw Frank Swift, massive and graceful, explain the art of goal-keeping. I remember vividly Swift catching the ball with one hand and holding it above the head of a tiny Barnsley forward who kept jumping for it like a dog for a bone. It was here I saw a stripling youth called Blanchflower spin the first delicate lines of his genius and looking incongruous as a thoroughbred in a donkey derby. Here too I saw Matthews and Doherty and Carter and Lawton and Mortensen and Shackleton. But great as they were, and glamorous too, I never loved them as much as the nondescripts who made up the Barnsley team throughout the years.

Watching football today I am constantly aware of the changes that have taken place, not so much in the game itself but in the actual physical appearance of the men who play it. Today's young men are sleek and streamlined, their hair stylishly cut, their faces slicked and smoothed with after-shave, their shorts minutely brief, their shirts moulded to their bodies. If you line them up there's nothing in their appearance to tell you who is the right full back and who is the inside right. Twenty years ago and less every player who came to Barnsley was built according to his position. The goalkeeper was always a light heavyweight, muscular but not muscle-bound. The full backs were short, squat men with prison hair-cuts, no-nonsense faces and fearsome legs. The centre half was always the tallest man in the side, with a forehead hammered flat through contact with a thousand muddy footballs, and flanking him were the wing halves, the frighteners, who were invariably built on the lines of dance-hall bouncers. The right wing was always small and fast, the left wing bandy-legged and tricky, the centre forward wore the desperate, haunted look of a man who was expected to run through brick walls and be roundly abused if he shirked it. The inside forwards invariably wore their hair a little longer than the rest and carried with them an air of intellectual superiority, like grammar school boys playing in a pit team. Throughout the years, every Saturday afternoon when it always seemed to be raining, this united collection of assorted human beings decided my mood for the coming week. If they won we went home chattering with excitement and the old man took the old woman to the boozer and I'd go to the cinema. If they lost, the trek to the bus station was like a funeral cortège the bus was a hearse and the report in that night's *Green 'Un* an obituary to a loved one. I last stood on that spot on the terrace in Barnsley eight years ago and since that time have seen football in many places. I have seen Real Madrid in Spain, Milan in Italy, I have travelled to games by gondola, air-conditioned Cadillac and private light aeroplane. But I have never got over

Barnsley. Once in Los Angeles I picked up an American paper which in small print said Barnsley 1, Stockport County 21, and I spent three worried days and sleepless nights until the rice-paper editions arrived to tell me that there had been a misprint and the game had been drawn.

There are, of course, thousands more like me; all I have done is to describe a symptom known to every man who ever gave his heart to a football team. I am luckier than most in that my therapy is in being allowed to write what I remember. This book is one man's very personal view of football. I have never cared for the game's theory—it would be too much in any case to expect a Barnsley supporter to appreciate sophisticated tactics—rather I have loved the men who play the game, trying to see them against the agitated background of an audience which drew sustenance from them. Some men went to soccer to simply stand for ninety minutes in the open air as a welcome change to a lifetime spent underground, others went to rid their frustration on someone who couldn't hit back, some went like myself because we were caught in a daft love affair which defied reason but gave us colour, movement, humour, drama and a million memories.

What follows are mainly memories, the rest are day-dreams.

The Players

'There are eleven players on a football field.
I know because I have counted them.'
Letter in 'The Times'

Necessary Screwballs

Goalkeepers, like things that go bump in the night, defy analysis. They are as much a mystery in the general order of things as the function of the human appendix. It is, of course, relatively easy to explain what they have to do: their purpose is to prevent the ball entering the net by any means at their disposal, namely by catching it, punching it, kicking it, heading it or, if they so desire, throwing their caps at it. The mystery lies in the fact that this seemingly simple, straightforward task produces people of incredibly complex and often eccentric personality. Even today, when the game appears to be played by robots, when individuality is ruthlessly stifled at birth, the goalkeeper has survived with all his personal idiosyncracies intact. No one knows better than goalkeepers themselves that the price they pay for their freedom is to be talked about behind their backs. In the totalitarian regime of modern-day soccer they are treated as necessary screwballs. Because of this it is a commonly held belief that all goalkeepers have a slate loose, that the nature of the job being what it is a man must be barmy to do it. The other theory is that the goalkeeper, because he is custodian of the most important part of a football field, slowly develops into a paranoiac.

I suspect that Clakker May would be regarded as a classic example by those people who reckon all goalkeepers are born crazy. You'd never suspect there was anything wrong by looking at him. He was a tall, stringy, quiet youth who lived with his parents and ten brothers and sisters in a council house near the pit gates. He became our goalkeeper quite by chance. One day we were a man short, and Len, our trainer, asked Clakker to play in goal. The result was a revelation. It wasn't so much when he donned the jersey he changed in his attitude towards his team-mates, it was simply that he believed that the rules of the game related to everyone except himself.

We became aware of his quirk the first time he touched the ball. He left his goal line to meet a hard, high cross, caught the ball cleanly, shaped to clear downfield, and then, for no apparent reason, spun round and fled to the back of the net. This move dumbfounded players, officials and spectators alike. As we stood gaping, Clakker ran from the back of the net and booted the ball over the halfway line. Nobody moved as it bounced aimlessly towards the opposite goal and then the referee broke the silence by blowing on his whistle and pointing to the centre spot. This appeared to upset Clakker.

'What's tha' playin' at?' he asked the referee.

'I was just about to ask thee same question,' said the referee. By this time Len had run on to the field.

'What the bloody hell . . .' he began.

'Nay, Len. Tha' sees I caught this ball and then I looks up and I saw this big centre forrard coming at me and I thought, "Bugger this lot", so I got out of his way,' Clakker explained.

'Tha' ran into t'bloody net wi' t'ball and tha' scored,' Len shouted.

'Scored,' said Clakker, incredulously.

'Scored,' said Len, emphatically.

Clakker shook his head. Len tried to keep calm. 'Look, lad,' he said, putting his arm round Clakker's shoulders, 'I know it's thi' first game and all that, but tha' must get one thing straight. When tha' catches t'ball gi' it some

'He was a mile off-side, wasn't he?'

clog downfield. Whatever tha' does don't run into t'net.'

Clakker nodded.

But it made little difference. In the next twenty minutes Clakker ran into the net thirteen times and we were losing 14—2. At this point the referee intervened. He called us all together and said: 'Na' look, lads, this is making mock of a great game. If it goes on like this t'scoor will be in t'hundreds and I'll have to mek a repoort to t'League Management Committee and there'll be hell to play.' We all nodded in agreement. The referee thought a bit and then said: 'What we'll do is amend t'rules. If Clakker runs into t'back of t'net in future it won't count as a goal, allus providin' he caught t'ball on t'right side of t'line in t'first place.'

Everyone agreed and play continued with this extraordinary amendment to the rules. At the final whistle we had lost fifteen to five and Clakker had shown that apart from his eccentric interpretation of the rules he was a remarkably good goalkeeper. Nobody said much after the game. It seemed useless to ask Clakker what went wrong because all of us agreed that like all goalkeepers he was a bit screwy. Our theory was confirmed by Clakker's old man, who when told of his son's extraordinary behaviour simply shook his head and said, 'He allus was a bit potty'.

But that was not the end of Clakker's career, not quite. He was picked for the next game because we didn't want to hurt him too much. Len, the trainer, called us together on the night before the game and explained how we might curb Clakker's madness. His plan was that the defenders should close in behind Clakker whenever he went out for a ball and bar his way into the net. Any resistance from Clakker should be firmly dealt with and if possible the ball taken from him and cleared upfield. In case Clakker should break through his own rearguard Len had taken the precaution of hiding the nets. His theory was that provided Clakker ran into goal, but straight out again, the referee would be unable to decide what had happened.

The reports of our last game had attracted a large crowd to the ground for Clakker's second appearance. All his family were present to see if it was true what people were saying about Clakker's extraordinary behaviour.

Things worked quite well for a time. Every time Clakker caught the ball we fell in around him and urged him away from his goal. Once he escaped us and nipped into goal, but he had the sense to escape immediately around the goalpost and clear downfield. The referee looked puzzled for a minute and gave Clakker a peculiar look, but did not give a goal because he could not believe what he thought he saw. We were leading two goals to nil with five minutes of the first half left when Clakker gave the game away. Over-confident at having duped the referee once before, he ran over his own goal line with the ball. His plan came to grief when he collided with the iron stanchion at the back of the goal. As he staggered drunkenly against the support the referee blew for a goal and gave Clakker the sort of look that meant all was now revealed.

When half time came none of us could look forward to the next forty-five minutes with any optimism. Len came on the field and beckoned myself and the centre half to one side. 'Na' look, lads, we've got to do something about yon Clakker,' he said. 'I've thought about playing him out of goal, but that's too dangerous. I can't just take him off because yon referee wouldn't allow it. So there's only only thing we can do.' He paused and looked at both of us.

'What's that?' I asked.

'Fix him,' said Len.

'Fix him?' I said.

Len nodded. 'When you get a chance, and as soon as you can, clobber him. I don't want him to get up, either,' said Len.

The centre half was smiling.

'Look,' I said to him, 'we can't clobber our own team-mate. It's not done.'

He looked at me pityingly. 'Leave it to me,' he said. 'I've fixed nicer people than Clakker.'

It took two minutes of the second half for Clakker to get fixed. There was a scrimmage in our goalmouth and when the dust had cleared Clakker lay prostrate on his goal line. Len came running on to the field, trying to look concerned. The centre half was trying hard to look innocent. Clakker's father had drifted over to the scene and was looking down at his son's body. 'He's better like that,' he said.

Len said to him, 'Tek your Clakker home and don't let him out till t'game's finished.'

Clakker's old man nodded and signalled to some of his sons to pick Clakker up. The last we saw of them they were carrying Clakker out of the field and home. We did quite well without him and managed to win. Afterwards in the dressing room some of the lads were wondering how Clakker became injured. Len said: 'Tha' nivver can tell wi' goalkeepers. It's quite likely he laid himself out.'

Clakker had a profound effect on me. Since that day many years ago when he was persuaded out of the game I have never been able to watch a football match without spending a great deal of the time wondering what was going on underneath the goalkeeper's cap. None of the goalkeepers I have ever seen in first-class football could hold a candle to Clakker, but most of them from time to time have revealed flashes of rare individuality. Bradford Park Avenue once had a goalkeeper called Chick Farr who thought nothing of racing far out of his goal area, tackling an opposing forward and racing off downfield like a demented Stanley Matthews. Whenever his little fantasy was interrupted by a successful tackle Farr would gallop back to his goal line, from time to time casting fearful glances over his shoulder like a man being pursued by a ghost. Farr's other party piece was strictly illegal. When he could not be bothered to save a high shot he would reach nonchalantly above his head and pull the cross-bar down. Faced with the inevitable telling off from a referee, Farr would pull his cap down over his eyes and try his best to look gormless. His act was a convincing one, not because he was born that way, but because like every goalkeeper he had become expert in hiding his folly. Occasionally, however, the stresses of the occupation become too much for some goalkeeper and they crack up. Sometimes it happens in public, as with the recent case

'Who are they playing, anyway?'

of a First Division goalkeeper who showed his displeasure at the way the crowd was criticising his goalkeeping by taking his shorts down and showing a large part of his backside to the terraces. At least this particular goalkeeper relieved himself in one great, spectacular gesture. The majority of his kind spend years suffering between the posts, whipping boys for the mob at the back of the goal, sacrifices to the inefficiency of their team-mates. I watched one goalkeeper at Barnsley suffer this way through many seasons. He came to the club fit and virile and stuffed with confidence. When he left on a free transfer he had shrunk inside his green jersey, his nerves were destroyed, they even rumoured that his wife had left him. I often wondered what became of him and discovered the truth sometime later when I was doing a story about a building site. I was talking football with the foreman when he asked me if I remembered the goalkeeper. I said I did and the foreman said he was working on the site.

'Where is he?' I asked.

'Up theer,' said the foreman, pointing towards heaven.

'Where exactly,' I enquired, hoping he wasn't trying to be funny.

'On top of yon chimney,' said the foreman.

I peered up, and there, high in the sky, sitting on top of the chimney was the goalkeeper.

'He seems to like it up theer. Can't get him down until it's knockin'-off time,' said the foreman.

I thought there might be a story in it, so I asked the foreman if I might interview the goalkeeper.

He shrugged. 'He's a funny bugger, but I'll try.'

He cupped his hands to his mouth and bellowed at the top of the chimney, *'Alf, theers a repoorter down 'ere what wants to interview thi abart goalkeepin'.'*

There was a long silence. Nothing stirred on the top of the chimney for a while and then the figure turned and looked down. And down the miles of silence separating us floated the reply:

'Tell him to get stuffed.'

The foreman shrugged and said, 'I told you. He's a rum feller. Still, I always think tha's got to be a bit strange to be a goalkeeper.'

I've often wondered since what kind of peace the goalkeeper discovered on top of that chimney, and wondered also what kind of revenge he was planning on the people below who had driven him there. I don't think he was potty or excessively anti-social. It was simply that he, like every goalkeeper, knew what it was like to be one of the world's most abused minority group.

2

Closet Wingers

It is an axiom of the modern game of football that wing-men, like people who thatch roofs and make clogs, are a dying breed. It is remarkable that a country whose one certain contribution to the international history of football is Stanley Matthews should now seem intent on pretending that he never existed.

Once upon a time in the days when footballers wore shorts to their knees and were shod in boots with bulging toe-caps the sight of the wingman improvising his talents down the touchline, delighting and disappointing in turn, was a commonplace on the football fields of Britain. Wingmen were the temperamental artists whose perform-ance was controlled by the state of the moon, or the horo-scope in that morning's *Daily Mirror* or more simply by the fact of whether or not they felt like playing well. They were the only members of a side who were allowed the luxury of personal eccentricity by the fans. I once played with a winger who wore a flat cap and woollen mittens on days when the weather was bad. Neither his team-mates, opponents nor spectators ever remarked his curious attire because he was a wingman. Had he been a centre half or a full back he would immediately have been marked down as a weirdo of some sort and asked to mend his ways or retire from the game.

In those dear departed days the best wingmen were

always referred to as closet wingers. It grew out of the days when we had the best team in the Barnsley and District Backyard League. Our success depended mainly on an unbeaten home record which was achieved by the efforts of our right winger, Albert, and a long row of outside toilets or closets as they were more commonly known.

Albert was an absolute master at charging down the wing and, when challenged by the opposing defenders, flicking the ball against the toilet door and collecting the rebound. The only time he was known to fail was on the occasion when the occupant of the toilet opened the door in time to take one of Albert's passes in the midriff.

Albert became well known locally as Geronimo, the closet winger. The Geronimo tag had nothing to do with his footballing ability but derived from his hatred of water and hair-cuts which created an appearance to remind us all of the Indians we saw on the screen at the local flea-pit. In those days our tactics were simple and effective. At every conceivable opportunity we would feed the ball to Geronimo, who was invariably lurking by his beloved closets, and away he would go, flicking the ball against the toilet doors, racing on to the rebound and repeating the act until he had cleared the whole defence.

For a couple of seasons we were unbeatable and Albert the closet winger became a local personality. Inevitably it couldn't last for ever and the slide downhill for both Albert and the team came on the day we met the Klondyke. The team was so named because the part of the village it represented put one in mind of a frontier town during the gold-rush. To describe them as hard opponents would be doing them an injustice. Ferocious is a more accurate description. They had at least two players who would make Mr. Norbert Stiles and Señor Rattin look like a pair of cream puffs.

It must also be remembered that in the Backyard League there was no referee to penalise dirty play. The simple ethic therefore was: 'If kicked say nothing, but wait and kick back.' Also in these games we did without the normal post-match formalities like shaking hands and congratulating the other chap. Any team which beat the fearsome Klondyke realised that when the game ended the sensible tactic was to race home immediately because any attempt at the normal courtesies would undoubtedly mean a free ride to the local out-patients department.

It was in this frame of mind we began our epic en-

'Delaney—from a free kick.' (By courtesy of *Punch*)

counter. All went reasonably well until Albert began his first run down the wing. In and out of the defence he went, flicking the ball on to the toilet doors, the rebound magically dropping at his twinkling feet. With the Klondyke defence nonplussed he shot home the first goal.

The Klondyke team, for all the fact that it included many players with surprisingly narrow foreheads and close-set eyes, were not short on swift answers when faced with a problem like this. The next time that Albert set off on one of his runs we were made aware of the Klondyke genius for tactical improvisation. As Albert twinkle-toed along the toilets, the Klondyke full back, built like a brick brewery, began a diagonal run towards him. As he reached Albert he didn't stop to challenge, he didn't hesitate to decide which way the winger was going, he just kept running as if his target was somewhere on the horizon beyond Albert's right shoulder. The noise of impact, of bone on bone, was terrible, and followed immediately by the sound of splintering wood as Albert, the full back and the ball smashed through one of the green toilet doors. We peered inside and the wreckage was awful.

Albert and the full back lay at peace on the floor, surrounded by fragments of wood and jagged pieces of what is politely termed sanitary ware. We picked them up and revived them and then had to abandon the match because the owner of the toilet turned up on his daily visit and when he saw the damage went to fetch the police. We never played there again because the law warned us off and some time later the council pulled the toilets down along with the houses they belonged to. The inhabitants were shipped out to a new estate with inside toilets and a better view of the pit. Albert went with his parents to the new estate, but he was never the same winger without a row of closets. After a couple of months in his new environment Albert went into premature retirement in a remand home for stealing lead. But he had made his mark. Whenever we saw a good winger he was always a 'closet winger'.

It is easy to scoff at closet wingers, but in fact they have made a colourful contribution to our game. What is more significant, it was a closet winger who unwittingly decided the future of English football. As is generally known, it was Sir Alf Ramsey who killed off the old romantic notion of wingmen. In Ramsey's team of workers there was no place for the eccentric or the whimsical. It was a beautiful machine and it didn't need adorning with frills. Now contrary to general opinion Sir Alf's plan for wingmen did

'Now then, who's got a pencil?'

not occur because he simply happened to think about it one day while taking a bath. It is my theory that his scheme for the liquidation of wingmen had lurked in his mind for some considerable time and had its roots in some kind of deep emotional upset. Which is where a closet winger called Johnny Kelly comes in.

He was a left-winger of genius who played for Barnsley in the early fifties. A shy, square sturdy man with the slightly bandy legs that are the hallmark of all great wingers.

I don't know if you've ever considered the remarkable fact that bandy legs are an asset to most sportsmen. That they help people who ride horses is a thought too obvious to need explanation. But it is not generally known that they greatly assist cricketers also. I once played in a cricket team with a man who possessed the most splendid pair of hooped legs I have yet seen.

As a batsman he was particularly skilled in the art of back play. Now this technique was generally suicidal in the league in which we played where the umpires worked strictly to licensing hours and granted leg-before-wicket appeals with increasing regularity as opening time approached. In this situation my bandy-legged friend was the only batsman in the league to play back and prosper. Whenever struck on his superbly bowed legs and appealed against he would simply point to the gap between his limbs, through which all three stumps were clearly visible, and say to the umpire in his most pained voice: 'Leg before wicket with a pair of bloody legs like mine?' No umpire, no matter how thirsty, dare give him out!

I digress only in the interests of science and humanity. It is time someone pointed out the virtues of playing sport on a pair of bandy legs. No one who has them should feel unhappy so long as they always remember to play back.

Which returns us to Alf Ramsey, because those of you with long memories will doubtless recall that he also used to play back—full back, that is—and very good he was too. But he was no good against bandy-legged wingers, as Johnny Kelly proved. Kelly was the kind of winger you don't see around nowadays. A player of skill and original wit. The sort of wingman who exploded theories, not expounded them. He played only once for Scotland, which was an act of criminal neglect on a player who must have been the best Scottish winger of his day. That he was ignored has obviously to do with the fact that he played for Barnsley. The selectors in Glasgow obviously thought they played in the Isthmian League. A great pity, because he had the kind of unique skill that should have been spread before multitudes and not just the faithful 15,000 who used to watch Barnsley in his day.

Still, it does mean that there were 14,999 other people who will swear to what I am going to tell you now. They and I were present that important day, many years ago, when Alf Ramsey suffered the trauma that changed his life and put the skids under wingers. He was playing right back for Southampton at the time, an urbane, immaculate footballer who seemed as out of place at Barnsley as a bowler hat in a pawnshop.

In this particular game Johnny Kelly had one of those days when all his genius flowed into his feet. If you have ever seen Matthews or Finney or Georgie Best at their finest then you'll know what I mean. He flicked his hips and Ramsey sat down in wonderment. He waved his foot over the ball like a wand, daring Ramsey to guess what might happen next, and as the full back anticipated a move outside, Kelly came inside and left him for dead. At one stage he demonstrated his complete mastery by beating Ramsey, waiting for him to recover and then beating him again. Had Kelly been on the Southampton side and doing this to certain of the Barnsley defenders he would have had his impudence rewarded with a bed in the nearest emergency ward. But Ramsey played it clean and endeavoured to look as dignified as any man can when he is having his nose rubbed in the dirt.

The crowd didn't help. They relished the sight of Kelly shredding Ramsey's reputation. This, remember, was in the days when footballers were the victims of individual abuse and not the collective sort they get from today's rehearsed choirs. Thus the comments, though not so loud, were more personal and biting. As Ramsey sat down before Kelly's skill a man near me bellowed:

'Tha' wants to learn how to stand up before tha' plays this game, Ramsey.' And again, as Kelly left Ramsey immobile and helpless as a statue, the same man bawled: 'Ramsey, tha' art about as much use as a chocolate teapot.'

This is as much as any man can be expected to take without consulting the Director of Public Prosecutions. My theory is that as Alf Ramsey sat in that dressing room in Barnsley, scraping the mud from his boots and his reputation, he first thought of his revenge on wingers. He didn't want just Kelly's scalp, but the destruction of the whole tricky race.

It's not a bad theory, particularly when you consider that Alf Ramsey is where he is today, and Johnny Kelly was last heard of manufacturing a liquid bleach. It's an even stronger theory when you realise that wingers like Kelly are now more rare than five-legged giraffes.

But I have cornered whatever consolation there is left to people who loved the game in the dear, daft days before Mr. Ramsey got his paws on it. When I read of the experts trying to explain to themselves just what he is up to, and why, I sit there giggling gently to myself, nursing my memories, thinking fondly of a grey afternoon many seasons ago when a closet winger with bandy legs and baggy shorts made a monkey of a master mind.

3

Memories are made of ...

Great inside forwards, like blissful marriages, are made in heaven. They are fashioned out of gold and sent on earth to win football matches and weave the stuff that memories are made of. Their deeds are branded on the mind. They are the architects who design a game, the artists who adorn it. Wingmen are more spectacular, centre halves more pugnacious, goalkeepers more idiosyncratic, but inside forwards, like leg-spin bowlers, are the connoisseur's delight.

My first clear memory of football is of a great inside forward at work. His name was Horatio Carter and I don't know how old I was when I first laid eyes on him, but I do remember that it was in the days when he played with Sunderland and he came to Barnsley and I stood on a tin can to see over the heads of the spectators in front of me. He strode alone on to the field some time after the other players, as if disdaining their company, as if to underline that his special qualities were worthy of a separate entrance. The Barnsley fans gave him the sort of reception they reserved for visiting dignitaries. You know the sort of thing: 'Big 'ed' and 'Get your bleedin' hair cut, Sybil'.

He treated the crowd and the game with a massive disdain, as if the whole affair was far beneath his dignity. He showed only one speck of interest in the proceedings, but it was decisive. The scores were level with only a few minutes to go when Carter, about thirty yards from the Barnsley goal and with his back to it, received a fast, wild cross. He killed it in mid-air with his right foot and as it dropped spun round and hit an alarming left-foot volley into the roof of the Barnsley goal. At least after he was seen to kick the ball it was seen to appear in the net, but no one on the ground, least of all the Barnsley goalkeeper, could say just how it arrived there. Carter didn't wait to see where the ball went. He knew. He continued his spin through 180 degrees and strolled back to the halfway line as if nothing had happened. Normally the Barnsley crowd greeted any goal by the opposition with a loud silence, but as Carter reached the halfway line a rare thing happened. Someone shouted: 'I wish we'd got eleven like thee, Carter lad.' The great player allowed himself a thin smile, as well he might, for he never received a greater accolade than that. In the following years I saw him whenever I could, first with Derby County, where with Peter Doherty he made up the most attractive and deadly pair of inside forwards possessed by any club side in post-war England. Then in his later years I watched him give his spectacular one-man show with Hull City. The sight of one man conducting the fortunes of his team is the most warming spectacle in football. It's an heroic situation in which the individual takes on the awesome qualities of the silent stranger in the cowboy film, the man who rides slowly into town and plugs all the baddies. Carter's performance at Hull contained all the heroic qualities, but they were embellished by the man's sense of showmanship. During the course of his weekly demonstrations of the art of football to the citizens of Hull, Carter took all the corners, all the free kicks, all the throw-ins, and, of course, all the penalties. Such was his domination that when one arrived at the ground one half expected to see Carter at the turnstile taking the gate money.

From the moment I first saw him at Barnsley, Carter became the first player in my World XI to meet the Outer

'*Good lad! . . . Now nip off home and tell your dad you've signed provisional forms for the United.*'

Galaxies. The curious thing about that team, which proves what I say about inside forwards, is that eventually the forward line consisted of three inside rights and two inside lefts: Horatio Carter, Len Shackleton, Ernie Taylor, Bobby Charlton and Steve Griffiths.

Of that bunch only Griffiths is unknown, but he was a marvellous footballer. I suppose in the few years he played with Barnsley he gave me more delight and taught me more about the inside forward's art than any other player. He learnt his skills in the South Yorkshire coalfield in the days when, if Barnsley were short of a player, they simply whistled down the pit shaft and took the first man up. Today if they whistled at the pit top the chances are they'd get a bass guitarist for a pop group.

Griffiths played for a while with Portsmouth, and then, after the war, returned to Barnsley for the epilogue of his career. In those last few seasons he showed us all his repertoire. He was a slight man, with a thin, sad face and slender, slightly bowed legs. Dressed in an ankle-length overcoat, muffler and cap, he became the sort of figure you see standing outside betting shops in Yorkshire pit villages. No one looked less like an athlete, but this was part of his deception. He would shamble round the field looking preoccupied and lost, like a man who suddenly remembers he has left the tap running at home.

But the moment he received the ball you detected his skill. Like all great footballers he could take a ball from any angle and lay it quietly dead at his feet. I can see him now, quite clearly, shoulders hunched, the ball at his feet, standing in mid-field, moving this way and that, tormenting the defenders, challenging them to anticipate his ideas, torturing the crowd into screaming 'Get rid, get rid'. And always at the point where even I, his dearest fan, was damning him for a fool, when the defence seemed to have been allowed time to build an impregnable wall, he would move. A quick body swerve past the man marking him, a shuffle, a change of feet and a thirty-yard ball trimming the turf to drop like a dead bird into the full stride of the wingman.

His wing partner in those days was a tiny Scotsman called Gavin Smith, whose speed was such that the club was rumoured to have erected special gates at the corners of the ground which were opened immediately Smith started one of his runs in case he needed a few extra yards

'Don't forget to get a postal order for the you know what.'
(By courtesy of *Punch*)

to brake in. He was an ordinary player, Griffiths made him look like an international.

Griffiths was generous with his colleagues. When Tommy Taylor, that fine centre forward so tragically killed in the Munich air disaster, first came into the Barnsley team it was Griffiths who nursed him through his growing pains. In one game he gave Taylor a goal with a stunning gesture. He set off dribbling through the defence and by the time he reached the goalkeeper the field behind was littered with bodies. Griffith taunted the goalkeeper into a fruitless dive, walked the ball round him, trapped it on the line and beckoned Taylor to come and push the ball into the net. He retired soon after and I missed him sorely.

In more recent times my greatest pleasure in watching football has been by another inside forward, Bobby Charlton. Over the past few seasons we have seen him at his peak. Every aspect of his game, the control, the judgement, the finishing, have been distilled, until what we are seeing now whenever Charlton takes the field is the quintessence of the inside forward's art.

His play is a unique blend of delicacy and power. There are the long swaying runs that seem to take him through an opponent rather than round him and there is the sudden ferocity of his shooting. Once in a game against Tottenham I saw him score a goal of such speed and beauty that no one who saw it will forget. As the crowd roared in ecstasy, Charlton rubbed the mud from his boots and walked back to his position, seemingly embarrassed by the ritual molly-coddling he received from his colleagues.

In a game now notorious for petty behaviour and childish conduct by the players Charlton is a monument of unruffled calm. When, as often happens, he is felled by a lesser player, he allows himself a pitying look in their direction. But that's all. Nothing more. It's the nearest he gets to displaying emotion, because he has the quality of self-control that is the exclusive gift of all truly great sportsmen. Matthews had it, so did Finney, and Bradman and Hutton.

The link between Steve Griffiths, Horatio Carter and Bobby Charlton is their mastery of their trade. Their reward is that what they achieved is remembered long after the day on which they did it is buried under the passing seasons.

Hands Across the Sea

'We are going to sell soccer like soap powder.'
American Soccer Administrator

To anyone who is football daft

4

How are things in Waxahachie?

There has been much public disquiet of late about the number of English soccer players who are being tempted to play in American soccer. As my colleague Desmond Dribbel has written: 'The grisly army of soccer knockers are saying that English stars are selling out to the Yanks.'

But not all English footballers are being tempted away from home and health by the American dollar. Some, nay the majority, are resisting the temptation, putting love of the old country before the desire for easy money.

As evidence I offer correspondence sent to this office by an anonymous sports lover in Barnsley. He says he found it under a cushion in a local billiards hall after the Barnsley players had finished training.

Barnsley F.C.
Barnsley, Yorks.

Dear Mr. Hackensack,

I read with interest your plea for English footballers to come to America and would like to offer my services. I am married with two children and play on the right wing. The reason I want to make a new career for myself is that things have come to a pretty pass in England, as we say in the old country. Ever since Alf Ramsey managed to win the World Cup without using wingers we have become redundant. They tried to redeploy me but I feel lost when

I am not dribbling up my flank. The wife feels the same as I do. I hope you realise our problem and can help.

Yours in sport,
Ernest Clog (right-winger)

Waxahachie Wanderers F.C.
Texas

Hi Ernest,

As we say hereabouts: You herded your problem to the O.K. Corral. Glad to have you with us. Don't gnaw your guts about being a winger. Ramsey, Schmansey, as we say hereabouts. Here's the dope on our club. Twelve months ago we started to build our stadium. Thirty million dollars it cost us. Yes sir. It stands today at the meeting of forty-seven freeways, one of the biggest, goddam it, *the* biggest and best stadium in the whole world. It seats seventy thousand folk and incorporates an underground popcorn factory and soft-drinks plant.

Our football pitch is 270 yards long and 120 yards wide. The players and their families live in the Soccer Communal Co-habilitation and Fun Centre built under the stadium. Here players and their families can relax, one mile underground, removed from the fears that bug the lives of normal people. Your quarters will include a hi-fi system, colour television, a mechanical cow and a split-level motorised bed for you and your wife. The bed is the greatest. It converts to a head-to-head-twin-single-divan when you are in training.

You will be offered a three-year contract at £5,000 a year and honorary membership of the Free Reformed Church of Waxahachie. Just so we can ignite the booster rocket under this deal, could you please send me details of yourself and your good wife.

Sincerely,
Cyrus Q. Hackensack
(president)

'*Forget last season, man!!* . . . *It's this season we need points!*'

Dear Mr. Hackensack,

Thank you for your letter. I am worried by one thing: your pitch seems very large. My wife feels the same as I do. Also my wife is worried about the motorised bed, which, you say, automatically becomes a head-to-head-twin-single-divan when I am in training. She says she prefers the method commonly practised in England where her bed stays in one piece and I sleep in digs in Blackpool.

Yours in sport,

Ernest Clog

P.S. Personal details following.

Dear Ernest,

One thing you and your wife have to get clear is that we do things differently in Texas. Sure, the pitch is extra large. This is a prestige pitch for a prestige club and don't you forget it. Also, although the game out here is called soccer, we intend to alter it a little to suit the American way of life. Our Audience Research Division has shown that reaction-wise English soccer is yawnsville for the average American fan. So O.K., let's bend it a little.

Here's the idea so far: if less than four goals have been scored in any ten-minute period the umpire can signal on to the field eleven circus dwarfs dressed as Beefeaters. The idea is that play continues normally but the dwarfs are allowed to interfere at will just to fun up the game a little. They leave the field after three minutes and the game continues. We call it Pee Wee Sockeroo and this way we aim for sport without tedium.

As for the bed and your wife's fears, all I can say is that myself and Belle have used one for years and are very happy. I have asked Belle to write Mrs. Clog personally to explain her experiences.

Sincerely,

Cyrus Q. Hackensack

Dear Mrs. Clog,

My husband Cyrus tells me you are worried by the bed. Don't be. Once you learn how to control it you will discover a deeper motivation for integration of your marriage. My husband tells me that in dear old England they still separate players who are in training from their wives and families. Send them to some place called Blackpool. What a barbaric idea, I do declare.

Many years ago our Psychological and Deep Motivation Research Unit discovered that this separation led to great emotional disturbances both on the field and off.

From their findings we invented the adjustable bed which swings to a head-to-head position when the player is in training. This way we achieved that blissful state of marriage we call separation without parting. I am sure once you have tried it you will enjoy it.

Could you sometime in the near future send me your measurements, as we would like to have your drum majorette's costume ready for you when you step from the plane.

Sincerely,
Belle Hackensack

Dear Mr. and Mrs. Hackensack,

I am writing this letter as my husband has gone to Blackpool and is not allowed to write letters when he is training. I have talked over the matter with Ernest and both of us feel that we cannot come to Waxahachie.

We would not like to live a mile underground and I don't fancy much having a mechanical cow in my kitchen. Also from my own point of view the bed is worrying. Ernest said it didn't matter, but I don't like these mechanical contraptions, and, anyway, I always knew my Ernest was in good hands at Blackpool with Mrs. Blewett in the digs.

Also being a drum majorette is not my cup of tea, as I don't think it would be good for the children to see their mother parading about in front of Americans.

My Ernest told me he didn't much reckon the idea of playing with dwarfs dressed as Beefeaters and also he felt he was a bit too old to be running about on a pitch as big as yours. He says that what you want on a pitch as big as that is men on scooters and then you call it Scooker. He's a one, my Ernest.

Anyway, he's talked it over with the club here and they have been very kind with him. They have given him a free transfer and we're thinking of opening a fish-and-chip shop at Cleethorpes.

If ever you are round that way look us up. You never know, they say there are lots of Yanks on the coast looking for oil. My Ernest says that if the oil they find is as good as some of the footballers that are going to America they'll be bankrupt in a year. But that's just his way of going on.

Yours in sport,

Elsie Clog

'Believe me, mate, you're not missing much.' (By courtesy of *Punch*)

5

Give it back to the Indians

Not every British footballer managed to resist the Americans. Many, lured by the prospect of easy pickings, seduced by the enticements of a highly professional business operation, crossed the Atlantic to spread soccer through a foreign land. They formed a curious bunch of missionaries. Some settled easily in a country which they had previously seen only on the movies. Others soon grew disenchanted with the celluloid dream. Such a man was Arthur Strongitharm. Arthur's education was cut short at the age of fifteen by an unscrupulous talent scout who persuaded him to abandon his studies for a career with a Second Division club. Arthur was encouraged in his folly by his father, who, in return for his support, was given by the club in question a free season ticket and two autographed footballs. Arthur never quite made the top of the ladder and was playing out the twilight of his career with a Fourth Division club when he was sold to a team in America. His letters from America to his old manager Herbert Johnson were collected and published by the well-known agent Batboot Hardboiled (Mr. Sixty Per Cent), who rightly calls them 'a moving document of our times, a tearful testimony of misguided youth'.

Los Angeles,
California

Dear Boss,

Arrived safely here after long and tiring flite. The food
was lowsy on the plane, this bird gives me a plastic tray
with a lot of lettis on it and I said to her what's this luv?
and she says breakfast sir and I said what does tha think
I am a rabit or summat. But she did not seem to cotton
on so I asked her for a fry up but it never came. Anyway
when we arrived there was all these people laid on with a
brass band and birds with white boots on waving flags and
things and all showting. I can't tell you what they was
saying because they was Americans. Anyway boss this
bloke stands up and meks a speech saying how happy he
was that a star like me had come to play with his club
and all that old clog iron. To here him talk you would
think I was Stanley Matthews or summat so when we
shook hands I told him. You know me boss how I like
things in the open so I said look cheef tha wants to be
careful wi t'build up, tha'll ave em expecting miracles.
And he said for fifteen thousand dollars we expect miracles.
I think he was joking but you can't tell with these Yanks.
Then I did an interview with this television bloke and he
was a right twerp. Ows Barnsley doing in the world series
he said and I told him last time Barnsley won a cup
America still belonged to the bloody Indians and that
shut him up for a bit. Then he asks wot it was like me
playing for England and I was going to stick him one on
for being sarky like when I saw he meant it. So I told him
how I got my leg done when I was on the verge of international honours and how Alf Ramsey had got a down on
me and how you told me it was either him or me so I came
to America. It is a bit worrying though boss that they
seem to have things a bit mixed up here thinking I am an
international and that Barnsley is a grate club like Arsenal
and all that. It makes me wonder whose been sending the
wrong word over here boss. I did not mention by the way

about sending the money back home for the gambling debts because that's nun of their business is it boss. I must close now boss as too much writing gives me a headache. I think I need glasses, give my love to the wife when you see her.

Yours in sport,
Arthur

'While I don't wholly approve, Mary, I sincerely hope you're using Burnley as a banker.' (By courtesy of *Punch*)

Los Angeles,
Tuesday

Dear Boss,

I have been in bed today with a sick stumak. It must have been something I eat because the food is lowsy all letis and things. Honest to god boss soon I will look like that bugs bunny. I keep asking for some fish and chips but they think I am joking and just laff. Last nite we were in this restrant me and this mexican winger I was rooming with and I ask for some fish and chips and the winger starts laffin. Now you know me boss I don't like people laffin for no reason like that so I said to him and what's up wi' thee gunga din and he comes back wi a crack about dirty british. So I go to stick him one on the chin end and this waiter sends for the manager and we both get slung and anyway I am not rooming with the winger anymore. I have nothing against people like him but they are different from us boss as you once told me when that French team came with there funny ways. Anyway boss then I went to this topless bar they have here where the barmaids dont have any blouses on. Honest boss they serve beer like that with no clothes on and its a right giggle boss not like anything they have in Barnsley. I had three beers and no more because you know me boss I dont drink too much when I'm in training and then this big droopy bird comes over and says that will be six dollars and I says you must be joking droopy drawers and she says the laff is on you bud if you dont empty the back pocket so I told her heres a dollar and give us a big kiss. So she goes away and comes back with this bloke who starts talkin like George Raft so I threaten to stick him one on when someone asks if I am the footballer from England and when I says yes then its alright because the boss here owns the club. From then on it was drinks all round. Anyway I had some crisps and think I must have ate the blue one because I was sick all today. As yet I have not kicked a ball boss but I am looking forward to showing them a few tricks. They are funny people boss and the food is not what I am used to. They are always braggin about how big everything is. They had me on the television the other night again and the man says how about Los Angeles then and I says its like Blackpool but worse and he makes some crack about the cute way I talk. And then he asks me about Johnson and I tell him you are the best manager I ever played under and he starts laffin. I am just going to stick him one on the chin and when he says it is the first time he knew that the president

'*Ignore them, Sam!*'

managed a soccer club and then I understood what he was talking about. Anyway they all liked me on the programme and are talking about having me on every week which will be nice for the beer money. Time to close now as my head is hurting me again and my stomach is suffering too. If you see my wife tell her I will send some money soon boss and will write as well.

Yours in sport,
Arthur

Los Angeles,
Calif.

Dear Boss,

Sorry I have not ritten before but what with traveling and playing and all that stuff I have been v. busy. What I could do with rite now is ten pints of journey into space we used to have at the local do you remember boss. Honest the beer in America is lowsy. It looks like lemonaid. The other night I said to this guy in the bar your beer is a laff and he said not so funny as your beer bud. So I said put your money were your mowth is father. And he said ten dollars says I can drink you under the table and I say O.K. so we started drinking. When we get to ten I realise I am in training and say to this guy I have to stop now but some other time when I am not in training I will drink you under the table and besides the beer is too gassy. And he calls me chicken so I stick him one on the chin end and go home. You know me boss how I don't like fighting and all that stuff but what he said was nasty. They are like that though the men. The women here are a bit better and I have met a few v. nice ones if you know what I mean boss. You remember that red head when we played Bradford well there was this girl the other night who was a dead ringer for her. I met her in this bar and she tells me she is married but her husband is a bum. The next day she says she will take me to a love-in and I thought it sounded v. nice so I said yes. Well boss you know me, I have seen some things in my time specially when I was in the army in Egypt like I told you once but this love-in beats the lot.

There was all these people dressed like red indians in this park all playing tom toms and wearing flowers stuck in there hare. Ayup jeronimo I says to one of them joky like and he looks at me and makes a nasty crack and I am just going to sort him when this red-head I am with takes me away to a tent. Honest to god boss it was a proper indian tent like you see on the films and inside all these people smoking and it smells like the inside of a maltees brothel. This bird I am with asks me if I have smoked pot and I said I have red all abowt you lot in the papers all abowt drugs and things and I had a good mind to tell the law. She says I am square and I say to her that the people there could do with a hare cut and some square bashing and anyway I am in training so I left her. They have funny ways of enjoying themselves boss.

So far we have played six games, won one, drawn two, lost three, not v. good is it boss. They are playing me out of position boss I told them I am a striker boss but they play me deep and I am not v. happy. Also the referees are after me. In the first match this referee tells us that every now and then we have to lie down on the field so they can put the commershuls in. Anyway we were playing this side and this big mexican is niggling me from the start and I tell him twice that he will get a nuckel sandwich if he doesn't stop his littel tricks. We go for this high ball and he thumps me in the neck and I am lying there and looking round for him to fix him when this referee says to me stop there for twenty sekonds and I said when I get the mexican he will stop down for a lot longer and he warns me not to try the funny business.

So anyway this mexican starts his tricks again so when he goes down in the goalmouth I stomp him where it hurts. The referee comes up and I said you can have a v. long commershul now mister cos he wont be getting up for some time and he said you can watch it on TV because I am sending you off. So I went and then I was suspended and fined. It was not fair boss, you know what these forin players are like. The money is v. nice and all that boss but sometimes I wish I was back with you and all the lads and the beer. I must stop now as my head is hurting through riting too much. Please rite and tell me abowt things at home and if you see my wife tell her I will send sum money soon.

Yours in sport,
Arthur

Los Angeles

Dear Boss,

I cant understand why you dont rite. When you transferred me you sed you would keep in touch and let me know how things were going like that business with the bookmakers and my wife. I have not herd a word and am wondering what has gone wrong. Since I last rote we have played three games and lost them all. Not v. good. They are letting me play my normal game now boss but I am not getting the servis I need to be the striker.

Also that leg injury the one you told me not to menshun when I came here is giving me some gip every time I try to turn and the crowd is getting on to me. They don't understand the British way out here and dont seem to understand that we invented the bloody game so who are they to tell me wot to do. Also I am in trouble with that bird I told you about the one with red hair who was a ringer for that one in Bradford remember. Well she keeps turning up and wont leave me alone. I have not told her I am married cos that is not her business and anyway I dont want to hurt her but she keeps going on abowt coming to live with me and how she loves englishmen and thinks I am kute. I keep seeing her cos I am lonely but it doesn't help any does it boss. Wot I am getting round to is to see if you will have me back if I come home. I know you have a good opinion of me boss cos I saw the letter you sent the yanks telling them how good I was so I expect you wouldnt mind me coming back for the start of the season Rite back soon please boss and let me now cos things are getting on top of me here rite now and I am homesick for you all.

Yours in sport,
Arthur

'Where to, ref.? ... The station?' (By courtesy of *Punch*)

Dallas,
Texas

Dear Boss,

I am getting a bit choked not hearing from you. I am writing this in a hotel room in Dallas which is where we played today and got stuffed 3—0. Honest to god boss this is a lowsy team you sold me to. A rite gang of cowboys. The goalkeeper is a blacky straight from the trees honest to god boss. Today I get this long high ball in the area so I shape to take it and then I let it go through to the keeper and he stands on his line like a chocolate bobby waving his hands and jumping up and down and screaming and so this centre forward nips in and ping its two nothing and we've no chance. So he comes at me his eyes rolling like them black and white minstrels we saw at Blackpool and tells me Im stupid and all that so I say to him have a banana king kong and keep the lip buttoned. After the match the manager goes for both of us but I don't care anymore boss. They can stuff the contract. Please rite back soon boss and say I can come home and play for you and the lads again. I am sure they will transfer me as they know I am unhappy and they know you wouldn't mind paying back the fifteen thousand they paid for me would you boss. I am very fed up boss. The food is lowsy and the americans get on my nervs with all their bragging. Also that red haired bird who was a dead ringer for that one in Bradford is pestering me. I told her about the wife and things but she said that doesn't matter becos she is a hippy or something and they dont believe in things like that. Honest to god boss I wish there was two of me one for her and one for the wife. If you see the wife don't tell her about the red head boss because you know her she would have my guts for garters.

Yours in sport,
Arthur

Los Angeles,
California

Dear Boss,

You havent ritten to me so you can get notted and what is more you are in deep trouble. They are after you and will have your guts for garters ha ha. They are very mad that you didnt tell them abowt my leg injury when you sold me out here and also they are wondering abowt that letter you sent in which you said I was a second Stanley Matthews and all that guff. In other words they think you are a conman and are not pleased with you and are going to fix you which is wot you deserve. They found out after the last game when I went for this ball and my leg went and the doctor looks at it and says gawd we bought a crippel and then they asked me and I told them about how I got done at Chesterfield and how the speshulist said no more football and you said the speshulist was daft or something. And then I told them how you found out abowt me and the booky and the ponies and how you said keep your trap shut abowt the leg and I will sell you to the yanks and we will make some brass. They are not blaming me so there. It is you they are after and are going to stick one on you. That's wot they say anyway. They have payed me off and I am living with that red head I told you abowt the one like the bird at Bradford remember so you and the wife can both get stuffed. They had me on television abowt it all the other day and I told them everything and they were very nice saying wot you had done was trading in human flesh so I hope your ears was burning cos now you know why. I thowt you were my friend once now I know you are a snake in the grass.

Arthur

Encampment of Peace,
San Bernadino,
California

Dear Mr. Johnson,

I am writing to you because Arthur speaks about you regularly particularly when he has turned on. I am the red-headed girl he told you about in his letters and I want you to know that we are both happy here where we have found peace together and the real meaning of life. You might be interested to learn how Arthur came to live among the beautiful people. Well, after he was released from his contract by the football club he spent several days getting stinking and was finally busted by a cop for fighting and spent several days in the can. I was waiting for him when he left the jail and I brought him to our Encampment of Peace. Here in our search for truth and peace we study the ways of the Hopi Indians. At first Arthur resisted our ways, he refused to wear the simple and traditional dress of the Hopi, rejected the blissful state of peace we attain through smoking marijuana. But now he is completely adjusted. He spends most of his days sitting cross-legged outside our tepee playing with his holy beads, and writing poetry which he plans to read at our next love-in. His simple, direct approach to the English language makes him a significant poet. Imagine him reading in his Yorkshire accent verse like this:

> Into the open all those who suck up the
>   benevolent narcotic cannabis,
> Attention, Forward, with mind dials
>   pointed.
> Assault.
> Hemp is the way.
> The goons prohibit a gentle healthful
>   pleasure.
> Disobey.

I realise you will find it difficult to appreciate that the Arthur you once knew could write verse as meaningful as that but he has changed. We are very proud of him here. He is the first drop out from the soccer scene and has benefited us all with his forthright thinking. He seems to have forgotten all about playing soccer although occasionally I will find him lovingly polishing his boots which hang from a pole outside our tepee. He asks me to say 'OOgawna' to you which is Hopi for 'peace' and wonders if you would be kind enough to ask his wife to send him the international caps he won as a schoolboy. He wants to wear one for his poetry reading at our next love-in. He reckons it might be a psychedelic thing to do.

yours until we all make love instead of war,
                    Macelon Rubinstrauber

Three Ways of Looking at It

'Two kinds of people watch football matches.
Those who pay and those who don't.'
Extract from Royal Commission into Crowd Behaviour

6

Gentlemen of the Press

You addicts who get your weekly fix every Saturday with the football results, and you who gobble up the match reports in the pinks and greens and Sunday prints, simply don't know the half of it. You are unaware of what we in the business call 'The Drama Behind the Score Line'.

The thought occurred, not for the first time, while reporting a game at Preston. The press box on this ground is huddled against the side of the main stand, so that one sees the game on one half of the field through a large glass screen, which is all very well except for the fact that a flaw in the glass not only multiplies the players by twos and sometimes four but also distorts them hideously. The optical illusions caused by this glass are quite breathtaking. The most spectacular occurs in the second half of most games, when, with the sun in a certain position, one can count eighty-eight players in one half of the field.

Reporting in these circumstances is hazardous and leaves the sports writer with no comeback but the obvious one when he is accused of taking a distorted view of things. His conclusions about what has really happened on the field of play can only be made after a chat with his colleagues, when the truth is decided on the principle of majority opinions.

Thus: 'Lawton to Spavin to Dawson, who scored?'

'No, Lawton to Godfrey to Dawson.'

'No, Godfrey to Lawton to Spavin.'

'No, Lawton to Spavin to Dawson.'

Which means, of course, that the Lawton/Spavin/Dawson combination must be the correct one because two people have shared the same optical illusion.

Preston's problem is mercifully quite unique. Reporting at other grounds poses a different kind of problem. At Bolton, for instance, the choice facing the sports writer is very simple: either he can sit in the press box or his typewriter can. But not both together.

But the greatest hazard in sports reporting is telephoning one's story. It sounds such a simple procedure. The sports writer picks up the telephone, calls his office and his story is taken down by a typist at the other end. But there stands in the path of this glorious scheme an organisation called the G.P.O., represented by an instrument commonly referred to as a telephone. Any sports writer will tell you as he sobs softly into his pint about the exquisite eccentricities of the British telephone system.

On one occasion I picked up a ringing telephone in a Manchester press box and the girl said she had a call for me from Northern Ireland.

'Jim?' said the man in Northern Ireland.

'No,' I explained, quite truthfully.

'Look, stop playing silly devils with me, mate. You're in enough trouble already,' he said.

'Jim who?' I enquired, patiently.

'Look, mate, five hundred words by ten past five. That was the deal. It's now twenty past and no story, if it's not here by half past then there's trouble.'

'Now look here . . .' I began.

'No excuses, Jim. Just remember what happened at Burnley,' he said, and slammed the phone down. I asked all round the press box for a Jim from Northern Ireland and everyone thought I was joking. I still haven't quite got over worrying about him and wondering what terrible thing did happen in Burnley.

Astonishingly, most young people coming into journalism have a desperate ambition to become sports writers. It is a dangerous dream and we who know the truth should do everything in our power to save these young fellows. In my cub days I knew a charming young man whose only flaw was an earnest desire to report football. Apart from anything else, the major obstacle between

'*There I was . . . prosperous little business . . . nice house . . . car . . . money in the bank . . . then I won this £75,000 on the pools.*'
(By courtesy of *Punch*)

him and his ambition was his eyesight, which made it impossible for him to see anything but a hazy blur at more then ten yards' range.

He was eventually given his big break, but reckoned without the jolly wit of people who frequent press boxes. As he couldn't really see what was happening he relied heavily on the advice of his colleague. When the crowd roared he would ask, politely, the significance of the noise. More often than not they told him that someone had scored. At half time after a goalless first half of quite stupefying boredom this young man had the score at 4—3 and a notebook crammed with crimson phrases. He was, of course, told the correct score later in the game, and sensibly, ever after, he forgot about football reporting. He looked around for a job in newspapers where bad eyesight counts for nothing and eventually became a television critic.

You might think that his colleagues in the press box were unnecessarily cruel. But I take the opposite point of view. I think they did him a great service. They saved him from the drab, draughty hours in slum conditions and spared him the tussles with our telephone system. They shielded him from the degradation of being pleasant to some directors of some football clubs who are taught at an early age that sports writers crawl from out of the woodwork at night and whose knowledge of the game is buried so deeply in the furthest parts of their skulls that it would take a brain surgeon to find it. That young man with the bad eyesight was rescued from that kind of fate. He doesn't know how lucky he is. Only one editor of my acquaintance had the right idea.

He would always ask applicants for jobs: 'Tell me, what do you want to do?'.

And if, as nearly always happened, the applicant said: 'I want to be a sports writer,' he would be bellowed from the editor's presence his ears soundly boxed with phrases like 'Fools write about football and dreamers about cricket. I have no use for either on my staff.' It would be wrong, however, to present him as the kind of man who was just anti-sports. He was even more violent with people who said they wanted to be film critics.

But even his system was not foolproof. One day a youth who had heard all about him, and was therefore ahead of the game, called to see him.

'Do you want to be a sports writer, sonny?' asked the editor.

'Never, sir,' said the youth.

'Thank God. When can you start,' said the editor.

Which is how I got my first job in journalism and how I come to be writing about sport.

I hope now that the football results on a Saturday night will carry a fresh flavour for you.

'*Well, as you know, the lads have been doing none too well this season . . .*'

FD—5

7

The Voice in the Crowd

Every Saturday when Barnsley were at home we'd pick up Arthur by the bottom boozer and take him to the match—a little furry man who sat in the back of the car in a quivering silence like a bespectacled mouse while the old man continued his monologue about how Barnsley would pulverise Rotherham.

The old man reckoned he was henpecked and had a helluva life with his missus. You could imagine it to look at him. He was put on earth to be everybody's rubbing rag. But he changed dramatically once he got to the ground.

Having paid his half-crown and settled on his favourite concrete step behind the goals, he became a fearsome mixture of R.S.M. Brittain and King Kong. He undoubtedly possessed the loudest voice ever owned by a human being, and this, coupled with an actor's sense of timing, made him a star attraction at Barnsley's home games.

He wasn't a witty phrase-maker, he didn't believe in the devastating aside, but his bellowed advice of 'Get stuck in' or 'Get rid' or 'Let him bloody rot' had the simple effectiveness of a battering ram. He wasn't unique. In those days every team had its Arthur, the belligerent customer who demanded value for his money and roared like a wounded animal when he thought he was being

sold short. Today things are different. The art of barracking has lost its individual voice and has been replaced with
massed choirs singing silly songs. Today angry dissatis-
faction is expressed not with a bellow of pain but by a
toilet roll curling upwards from the Spion Kop, thrown
by a yobbo who can't think of anything to say.

The reasons for this change in social behaviour are for
someone else to explore, but the effect of the change

*'Excuse me, ref, my colleagues and I would be grateful if you would consult
the linesman about the legality of that goal.'*

saddens me. The lack of individual voice means a loss of
personal identity. Crowds today speak with the same
tongue no matter who they are supporting.

Football choirs throughout Britain all sing 'Yellow
Submarine', whether it be in praise of Millwall or South-
port, and even when a resourceful group breaks through
with something unique and personal, such as Liverpool's
'Ee-aye-addio', it soon becomes adopted nationally and
commonplace.

Where today are those strong, loud voices of individual
protest, the Arthurs who every Saturday found that the

Kop was their stage, where they broke free from nagging wives and bum bailiffs and for ninety minutes told the world and their fellow men exactly what they thought about them?

Barracking today has become the opposite of what it was intended to be. It is now a form of sing-song employed by spectators to entertain themselves when they are bored, instead of being the barb to goad the players and the spectators into new life.

That marvellous writer H. D. Davies would be horrified by today's crowds. He was the first football writer to spot the value of the lone persistent voice from the Kop. A few weeks before his tragic death Don Davies recorded the judgement of one critic at Maine Road on a winger who fancied himself as another Matthews.

After a thwarted attempt to weave his way through the opposing defence the winger was assessed by one spectator thus: 'Look at 'im trying to dribble. Why doesn't he learn? He's got nothin' else to do.'

Cricket, too, is suffering from much the same malaise as soccer. What it lacks today is the individual flash of perceptive barracking that means so much to the game. In Yorkshire and Lancashire, where this tradition was born, each team, whether it be the county side or the local XI, would have at least one outspoken critic whose self-appointed job was to scourge both locals and visitors alike.

Barnsley Cricket Club had such a spectator who every home game, no matter what the conditions, would sit, wrapped in a large brown raincoat, by one side of the sight-screen bellowing advice. No one escaped him. He was particularly fond of baiting our captain, a spiky old professional with a brittle temper.

On one occasion we were being trounced by the visiting team, and every time the ball flashed through our captain's defensive field placings for yet another boundary the man by the sight-screen would bellow, 'Put a bloody man theer.'

This went on for some time, until finally the skipper could bear it no longer. As the ball raced yet again to the boundary he stood with hands on hips facing his accuser and awaiting the inevitable. It came: 'Put a bloody man theer.' Our captain went purple and bawled across the field, 'How many men does tha' think I've got, sithee?' A pause, then back came the hoarse reply, 'Not bloody sufficient.'

Their feud was a constant feature of our games, and I believe in the end they became quite fond of one another. Their most memorable repartee occurred one day when we were faced with a large score on a very wet wicket and had decided to play for a draw. The captain tried to assure the result by wasting as much time as possible.

After every ball he would go down the wicket and indulge in extensive gardening. Being a fairly violent man by nature, he did not tap the divots back but thumped them into position with a resounding noise. He had just completed one of his sessions and was strolling back to his crease when the critic spoke.

'Ayup,' he bellowed. The captain turned to face him and shouted back, 'And what's tha' want?' The critic rose from his seat and replied, 'Tha' wants to be careful wi' all that thumpin', there's men workin' under theer.'

The captain and his critic have long since departed and there is nothing in their place except silence. I'll bet Don Davies's man at Maine Road now spends his Saturday afternoons in the betting shop and that the crowd at Barnsley nowadays is too busy remembering the words to 'Yellow Submarine' to invent anything quite so graphic as a 'chocolate teapot'.

The sadness of it all, the quantity of loss, was made apparent to me the other day when talking to a friend of mine who in his youth supported Chesterfield. He recalled the great days, but the interesting point was that he remembered the vitality and agitation of the crowd as much as the deeds of his heroes.

One of his collections will serve as an epitaph to the disappearing barracker. Chesterfield at the time had a fine inside forward called Tommy Capel, whose brother also played at full back. It was generally supposed by the Spion Kop fraternity that the full back made the side because of his brother's skill.

This feeling was given expression after one game, a cup-tie at Chesterfield, which the home team desperately needed to win. With the scores level and one minute to go Chesterfield were awarded a penalty. The kick was entrusted to the full back, the mistrusted brother. This unfortunate fellow took the penalty and not only missed by a mile but suffered the indignity of seeing his shot hit the scoreboard.

There was a stunned silence from the home fans, broken eventually by a lone voice from the Kop which, with immense dignity and suffering, declared, 'It's bloody nepotism, that's what it is, bloody nepotism'.

8

Gonk

The day we played Arsenal in the Cup in London was the day the Copper came round to see Gonk's old man. Gonk was not present on account of he was in a remand home for stealing lead.

'He's gone,' said the Copper.

'Allus knew he would. Doesn't have a ha'porth of sense. A right bleedin' birdbrain,' said his loving father.

'Just walked out early this morning. They asked me to come here to see if he was at home,' said the Copper.

'Wouldn't come here. Hasn't got the sense,' said his old man.

'If he comes give us a ring,' said the Copper.

'Quick as a flash,' said Gonk's old man, putting his drinking boots on.

Barnsley lost the cup-tie. It was the game when Skinner Normanton broke his leg. Skinner was Gonk's hero. They were very much alike, except Skinner was straight and Gonk was so bent he had to sleep on corrugated sheeting.

Sunday lunchtime, just when we are waiting outside the boozer and getting ready to charge the door down, Gonk comes walking down the road, looking tired and dishevelled.

'Ayup,' said his old man, looking at Gonk as if he was the rent collector.

'Ayup,' said Gonk, sitting on the wall.

'T'Bobbie's been and he tells me thar skipped it,' said the old man.

'Had to,' said Gonk.

'What for?' said the old man.

'To see Barnsley play, of course,' said Gonk.

'Football daft,' said the old man.

'I'm turnin' miself in,' said Gonk.

'Why?' said the old man.

'Skinner got done. Broke his bloody leg, they did. And we lost. Nothing else to do but go back, then, is there?' said Gonk, and off he went to find a copper.

There can be few football followers who have broken out of prison to keep faith with their idols. And more than that, walked to London and back to see Barnsley. I always thought they didn't make them like Gonk any more until I spent a few days in Liverpool and (I am willing to bet) from my various researches in that incredible city that Liverpool F.C. has more Gonks than any other team in the land.

I am also pretty sure that now he's living there under an assumed name. I base my theory on a reader's letter in *Kop*, an excellent and lively newspaper printed weekly for the delight of the Liverpool supporters. I reprint it without comment:

I am a young housewife who used to follow Liverpool but now with my little boy to look after leave it to my husband. I would like to nominate him for Fan of the Year. Here are the facts:

Our house is called 'The Kop'. Our sitting room is 'the Anfield den'. He has a lounge full of football pennants.

If Liverpool win we receive six Sunday and six Monday papers and all the cuttings are stuck in a scrapbook. He has a fantastic collection which no one dare touch because he says that one day they will be 'priceless'. If Liverpool lose there are no papers in the house and no lunch.

If they are playing an away match that he cannot get

'How'd you like a run at centre forward on Saturday?' (By courtesy of *Punch*)

to he wears red socks, red hat, scarf, tie and cardigan in the house as he waits for the result on the telly.

We have called our son after Ian St. John.

He interrupted our honeymoon to get back for the vital championship games in 1964. After the victory we returned to our honeymoon hotel.

When Everton lose he dances.

He calls the team 'the red gods', the ground is 'Anfield Arena', the opposition are 'sacrificial offerings', and Bill Shankly is 'the Emperor'.

Signed: Mrs. Pauline Griffiths

After reading that letter even I, incurably ill as I am with hereditary football fever, reckon that Mrs. Griffiths has found herself a rare one. She should ask her husband immediately if he had a nickname in his youth.

It was also in *Kop* that a writer summed up the wit and charm of the kind of man who sits in front of the telly dressed in his football gear waiting for the results. Recalling one game at Anfield the writer told how the opposing team's full back was having an awful match.

The longer the game progressed, the more hideous his incompetence became. The Kop treated him kindly until, near the end, the full back ran behind the goal to fetch the ball, his afternoon's labour summed up for him thus:

'Hey, you. I've seen better backs covered in dandruff.'

This story, in turn, revived my memory of a letter I once received from a man in Liverpool. I had written rather scathingly about the lack of crowd-wit on our football grounds today and was soundly taken to task by the writer.

He backed up his point of view with the following story: During the World Cup he went to Goodison Park, Everton, to see the Hungarians play Brazil. Albert, the Hungarian centre forward, had a marvellous game and was immediately adopted by the Liverpool fans. My correspondent was standing among a group of Albert's

keenest supporters when the centre forward did something
extraordinarily clever.

After the applause had died down a man in the crowd
was heard to say in a thick scowse accent: 'That Albert's a
good 'un.' There was a pause as he collected his super-
latives together and then he spoke his feelings:

'Do yer know, if I came 'ome and found 'im in bed with
the missus I'd take 'im an extra blanket and a cup of tea.'

Neither the correspondent nor myself have the slightest
doubt that he meant it.

*'If the Rovers and the Wanderers lose we should just avoid relegation
provided we win by eleven clear goals.'*

The World Cup

It must be said at once that England won the World Cup in 1966 without my assistance. Indeed, I was never nearer than a thousand miles to Wembley during the whole affair. This did not, however, stop me from expressing an opinion. At the start I was opposed to Sir Alf's ideas. I was proved wrong. What I discovered was that it is easy to hide one's shame a long way from the scene of the crime. Whereas in Britain I would have been asked to eat humble pie, abroad I was able to play the conqueror without even a momentary flicker of conscience.

9

Encounter in Tunisia

I knew it was going to be a funny sort of day when I received the message from the airline. It said, 'Please go to Tunis Airport to collect your dog which has arrived from Frankfurt.'

The only dog I ever knew at all well was a whippet we once had. We entered it once in a race just outside of Barnsley and after it had set off it never came back. We last saw it heading towards Wakefield. If this was the dog at Tunis Airport then it would be twenty years old and very tired.

I didn't dare ring the airport, though, just in case. So I sat in the hotel lounge and sneered at the Germans.

'Who won the World Cup then?' I gaily asked a man sitting nearby and reading a German paper which said that Germany were the real victors.

'You're so goddam superior, you British,' he said, with a slight American accent.

So I thought I'd go and meet the real Tunisians. They at least were pleased that we had won. The taxi-driver turned to me and said: 'Alf Ramsey definitely number one.'

It was an arrow shaft straight to my conscience. He meant well, of course, but he didn't know the hurt it caused me. So far everything indicated a drink, so we stopped at a roadside café outside of Tunis. We were joined by two men, one very big and very black, the other small, slim and very attentive to the other. He handled him like a manager fussing a prize-fighter.

'He used to be called the Pelé of Tunisia,' the small man said to us, indicating the large black man.

'How very nice,' I said.

'Well, he always really wanted to be Bobby Charlton but he thought people might laugh,' the manager explained.

The big man stirred. 'Charlton definitely premier. Pelé kaput.' He slid his finger across his throat.

'He's seen all the games, you know,' said the manager. 'Couldn't keep him away from the set. At first he wanted Brazil to win but after they lost he settled for England.'

The big man stirred again. 'England number one. Alf Ramsey plus plenty brains,' he said, and slumped back in his chair quite exhausted by his reasoning.

'What he means is that England seemed the most intelligent side. He read in one of the local papers about Bobby Moore and Nobby Stiles and he thought with intelligence like that they must win.'

'What about Bobby Moore and Nobby Stiles?' I said, wondering if some aspect of their character had evaded me.

The big man lurched forward again. 'Bobby Moore, ambassador to Paris. Nobby Stiles, son of British lord,' he said definitely.

'Oh yes it's true,' said the manager. 'It was in one of the sporting papers that Bobby Moore had a job in the Embassy at Paris and that Stiles came from a titled family. I am surprised you didn't know.'

I smiled weakly. More drinks appeared.

'Show the gentleman your legs,' the manager said. The big man stood up and flexed his thighs until his trousers began to creak.

'Feel,' he said indicating his legs. They felt like granite.

'Very impressive,' I said.

'He's very strong, you know,' said the manager. 'And

'Still, look what we're saving on bonus money!'

FD—6

he had lots of ambition. But things have been against him.' He looked all around him and then leant closer. 'You won't believe this, but his parents were white.'

'Really,' I said.

'As white as you, sir. And look at him. It really is remarkable, is it not?'

'Very,' I said.

The big man had been watching us while we were talking. 'Me white, me Bobby Charlton. Me black, nothing.' He shrugged his huge shoulders.

'It would have been all right if Portugal had won then he could have become Eusebio,' said the manager. 'But as it is. . . .' He too shrugged and ordered another round.

We all stared moodily at our drinks for a long time. I thought they looked unhappy, so I asked a gay, intelligent question. 'What position does he play?' I inquired.

They both started laughing. Not just gentle laughter, but great torrents of the stuff. I looked about me to see what was funny, but both my neighbours and myself seemed properly attired and eminently unhilarious.

'The skills of your game,' they confessed, 'have eluded him.'

And, still laughing, they stood up together and staggered into the night. It really was a very odd scene. It was even odder when I came to pay the bill and discovered they had been drinking all night on my account.

I have a faint suspicion that my creditable sporting pride may have been ruthlessly exploited. It was expensive; but I still went to bed feeling like a world champion.

10

Retreat in Malta

Much as it grieves me to return to the World Cup, you must understand we of the international jet set really can't escape it. If the celebrations have cooled in Britain there are other places throughout the world where they are only just warming up. For instance I had just arrived in Malta when the phone rang.

'Michael Parkinson?' the voice enquired.

'Yes,' I said, modestly.

'The one who writes that funny stuff in the *Sunday Times*?' the man asked.

'I have been referred to in that manner before,' I said, enjoying the cut and thrust of our conversation.

'Well, we'd like you to appear on our commercial television and give your frank opinion of the World Cup and Alf Ramsey,' he said.

I, of course, agreed. This was a gift from heaven, the chance to get the phlegm off my chest, to say one or two things about Alf's England that have been simmering gently in my brain ever since we won that cup. 'In the unlikely event of a fee, you should pass it on to the friends of Alf Ramsey Society,' I said in my most jocular manner. He is going to need it after this, I thought.

I prepared myself carefully for the interview, humming gently to myself the while. The face in the bathroom mirror was, I thought, the sort you see in the petrol ads—

lean, tanned, wordly wise. Slightly soiled, perhaps, and going a bit round the edges, but good enough for Malta television. I questioned myself as I shaved.

'Tell me, Mr. Parkinson, what do you think of England winning the World Cup?'

'Now I am glad you asked me that question. First of all let's take Alf Ramsey—and the further you take him the more I'll be pleased' (I paused here for imaginary laughter from studio technicians). 'Seriously, though, I think Alf should go a long way—Australia perhaps.'

'And how do you sum up England's performance?'

'As a classic example of how to win cups and lose friends.'

'Is any player worthy of special mention, Mr. Parkinson?'

'Roger Hunt. Throughout the tournament he turned in displays of quite staggering mediocrity. If talent was measured in elastic Roger Hunt would not provide sufficient material to make garters for a one-legged sparrow.' (More studio applause.)

I gave myself a little sign-off leer and winked at the camera in the manner of sports experts on the telly. I felt fine.

I whistled all the way to the taxi. At the studio I was met by the man who was to interview me, the local football expert. A kind of Maltese Kenneth Wolstenholme, if you know what I mean.

'What shall we talk about?' he said. I told him all the stuff I had told the mirror, all about Roger and Alf and the rest of that miserable English team.

'You can't say that on my programme,' he said, when I had finished.

'Why?'

'We'd never leave the building alive, old chap, that's why,' he said.

'You're joking,' I said.

'I'm not,' he answered.

'But in England I can call Alf Ramsey names without getting stoned. Why can't I do so here? What's the matter, has got local influence or something?' But the Maltese Kenneth Wolstenholme did not seem interested any more. He was chinning away to some water-polo player. I slumped in a corner feeling disenchanted. But after a while my training as a fearless reporter came struggling to the surface. 'Publish and be damned', I said. 'The man

'*Good luck.*' (By courtesy of *Punch*)

they can't gag' was another ringing battle-cry I remembered from somewhere or other. 'Go out there, Parky, and give 'em hell.' I squared my shoulders and braced myself for the interview.

The programme started. All of Malta was watching, or so I was told. The Maltese Kenneth Wolstenholme introduced me in his native tongue. I don't know what he said really. All I caught was 'Michael Parkinson . . . sport of . . . *Sunday Times* London . . . Twenty Four Hours.' Then he turned and said: 'Mr. Parkinson your impressions of the World Cup, please?' As he said it I thought of the rioting, of the mobs storming Television House.

'Very nice,' I said.

'And what about Alf Ramsey?' he asked, trying to rile me.

'Alf Ramsey for President,' I replied, blandly.

'And finally, Mr. Parkinson, where does English football go from here?'

'Forward, ever forward,' I said.

'Thank you and good luck.'

'Thank you and good luck to you, kind sir,' I said.

The director came into the studio and said it had been a marvellous interview. At any rate no one had rung up to complain which was always a good sign. 'At least you won't get stoned,' said the Maltese Kenneth Wolstenholme as I left. In the text I considered the significance of my noble gesture. For a moment the well-being of a nation had rested on the tip of my tongue. Mob law had been at my disposal. But I was right to do what I did. Not even the thought of fixing Alf Ramsey could persuade me otherwise.

Back in the hotel the face in the mirror seemed somehow different. Less raffish, more responsible, the sort of face that fits under a pith helmet. I wondered how I'd shaped up in my new job. Whistling the theme from *Lawrence of Arabia*, I went blissfully to bed.

The Game's the Thing

'Twenty-two men in tiny shorts running about trying to kick a ball into a string bag. And people pay to watch them. It's laughable.'

Collected Sayings of My Wife

Skinner

Cup-ties were different from other games. If Barnsley won we went to the pictures in the best seats, but if they lost there was sometimes a punch-up and the old man would come home from the boozer with a skinful saying the beer was off.

Barnsley, of course, used to be a good cup-fighting side. They only won the Cup once and that was in 1912, but they've never forgotten it and many a team from a higher division has been slain by them on that ground with the muck stacks peeping over the paddock. The reason for Barnsley's success in the Cup was, more often than not, that their game remained unchanged throughout years of tactical innovation. The team was both blind and deaf to subtleties like the bolt defence, the wall pass, 4—2—4 and deep-lying centre forwards. Their game was founded rock solid on two basic principles best summed up by the exhortations of their supporters to 'Get stuck in' or, alternatively, 'Get rid'.

During one spectacular cup run after the war, when Barnsley had beaten a First Division side, the old man held forth on the team's virtues on the bus going home. What he said was: 'They'll take some stopping, yon team. They'll kick 'owt that moves.' The bus agreed.

This love of hard combative graft above all else was not in any way unique among the supporters who Saturday after Saturday had their weekend-end mood dictated by how their team fared. Their unanimous favourites were the hard men who got stuck in and got rid without thought for the game's niceties. The odd sophisticates who crept into the team were tolerated but never loved. Thus they will tell you even now that Danny Blanchflower once played for Barnsley, but that he wasn't a patch on Skinner Normanton.

Normanton, I suppose, personified Barnsley's cup-fighting qualities. He was tough, tireless, aggressive, with a tackle as swift and spectacular as summer lightning. In the family tree of football his grandfather was Wilf Copping, his godson is Nobby Stiles. And just in case anyone is still uncertain about what kind of player he was, he could claim a distant link with Rocky Marciano. He was a miner and built like one. Billiard-table legs and a chest like the front of a coal barge. He was so fearsome that there are those who will tell you that naughty children in and around Barnsley were warned by their parents, 'If you don't be good we'll send for Skinner.'

The other legend about him, probably equally true, was that certain inside forwards of delicate constitution were known to develop nervous rashes and mysterious stomach disorders when faced with the prospect of a Saturday afternoon's sport with Skinner in opposition.

Cup-ties were his speciality, inside forwards with international reputations were his meat. He clinched one game for Barnsley in a manner all his very own. There was about ten minutes to go, the scores level, and Barnsley were awarded a penalty. The inside forward placed the ball on the spot and as he turned to walk back Skinner, from the halfway line, set off running. The inside forward, ready to turn to take the kick, saw Skinner approaching like an odds-on favourite and wisely stepped aside. From that moment the grey, dour ground was lit with the purple and gold of pure fantasy. Without slackening speed Skinner kicked the ball with his toe-end. And, as he did, many things happened: the bar started shaking and humming, the goalkeeper fell to his face stunned and the ball appeared magically in the back of the net. What in fact had happened was that Skinner's shot had struck the underside of the crossbar, rebounded on to the back of the goalkeeper's neck, flattened him and ricocheted into the goal.

'Sid, I wish you wouldn't bother trying to explain the off-side rule.'

Barnsley, by virtue of Skinner's genius in scoring with the penalty and at the same time reducing the opponents to ten men, won the game.

It was soon after, though, that Skinner for the first and last time met his match. Again it was a cup-tie and this time Barnsley were playing Arsenal at Highbury. Going down on the train with the crates of light ale under the seat, we agreed that if Skinner could frighten them Barnsley had a chance. But we didn't know that Arsenal had someone just as hard as Skinner and twice as clever. His name was Alec Forbes and Barnsley lost. Going sadly home, we agreed with the thought that if Barnsley had

Forbes they'd soon get into the First Division. What we left unsaid was that they'd probably make it by default because other teams faced with the prospect of playing against a side containing both Skinner and Forbes would probably give Barnsley two points to stop at home.

Anyway things have changed now. Skinner has retired and there's no one to take his place. The last time I saw Barnsley in a cup-tie things were different. They played Manchester United at Barnsley and went down ever so politely 4—0. United played as if they had written the modern theory of the game and Barnsley as if they'd read it backwards. There were no fights either on or off the field, Denis Law shimmered like quicksilver and scored as he pleased, and a young lad called George Best played with the instinctive joy of a genius. There was only one flash of the old fighting spirit. As Law cheekily and magically dribbled round the wing half, stopped, showed him the ball, then beat him again, a bloke standing near us shouted, 'Tha' wouldn't have done that to Skinner, Denis.' Those who remembered smiled. But knowingly.

12

The International

We put the beer in the boot and set off. We hadn't got a ticket but we didn't care. In fact, there were only five on the bus who had tickets. The rest of us were hoping to buy them outside the ground. By the time we'd reached Barnet the boot was empty and we were all feeling like Flash Gordons. London was ready for us. Everywhere there were signs of the International. One man was selling tartan hot-dogs, or so he claimed. We headed for Soho. It seemed the natural thing to do.

Jamie, who came from Glasgow originally, said we'd get some tickets if we hung around. We stood on the street corner trying to look like football supporters. Jamie had a rattle and I had a rosette.

A man came up to us and said:

'What do you boys want?'

Jamie said: 'Some tickets.'

The man said, 'For what?'

Jamie looked at him carefully and said, 'We'd not really made our minds up. What's on offer?'

The man looked about him and then said quietly: 'Anything you want, boys. Film shows or just a get-together. You've got the money, I've got the set-up.'

Jamie said: 'We are police officers in disguise. . . .' The man was gone.

We went into a likely looking pub for some sandwiches

and a drink. It was full of Scotsmen. The landlord couldn't make his mind up whether or not to be pleased. He obviously appreciated the trade but seemed as if he anticipated a riot at any moment. A man wearing a Tam O'Shanter came up to me and said: 'I'll buy your ticket.' I said I didn't have one. He put a pound note on the table and said: 'That's my last offer.'

I said: 'Look I don't have a ticket.'

He said: 'Are you looking for trouble?'

I said: 'You wouldn't hit a fellow countryman, would you?'

He looked at me suspiciously. 'From Scotland?' he asked.

'Edinburgh,' I lied.

He left it at that and went back to his seat. From time to time I caught him looking across at me, and when that happened I raised my glass and toasted him. When we left he was asleep and the landlord, as happy as a wet weekend, was trying to wake him up.

Jamie said to the landlord: 'Let him lie there. If you wake him he might come out fighting.'

The landlord said: 'Always the same. Savages.'

I grabbed Jamie's arm and pulled him out of the pub.

It was late afternoon, so we went to the cinema and had a sleep. When we came out it was evening and Soho was full of football supporters, all down for the big game, all looking for some unique method of getting rid of their money.

We settled for one of the more tried and trusted methods and very soon were a couple of merry football fans.

That night we slept in the bus in the car park because we couldn't find a hotel. Early in the morning a bobby looked in and said: 'Where are you from, lads?' And we told him Barnsley and he laughed and said: 'Take it easy.'

Even now I don't know why he thought coming from Barnsley was funny.

We went to the ground early to get some tickets. There were plenty floating around but they all seemed to be in the hands of seedy gentlemen in large overcoats who were asking outrageous prices. Two very large Scottish supporters came up to us and asked us if we were interested in taking one of the ticket-sellers down an alley and doing him over.

We thanked them for their kind thought but said we were waiting for our old man who was arriving soon on a police horse. They gave us a funny look and left.

We decided to wait until near kick-off time in the hope that the spivs would drop their prices. As we waited we watched the lucky ones with tickets arrive. Jamie said: 'Have you noticed that from what we have seen the average British football fan who gets a ticket for the international match wears a camel-hair overcoat, smokes a twelve-inch cigar and drives a white Jaguar?'

I nodded. 'In fact,' he said bitterly, 'it could be argued that people with rattles and rosettes who stand the goals every Saturday are the people who get locked out of the big games.'

With about five minutes to kick off we approach this spiv. He wanted six quid for a ten-bob ticket. We were still arguing when we heard the game start. We argued for another ten minutes, but the spiv would not drop his price. In the end he tore up a ticket in front of us, saying he'd rather burn them than sell them for less than a fiver We thanked him for his co-operation and headed back to Soho.

When we got on the bus going home that night we didn't tell the rest of the lads that we couldn't get a ticket. We pretended we had seen the game and when we arrived home we told everyone how we argued with this spiv until we got two ten-bob tickets for a quid, and what a game it had been.

In fact we had both paid out ten quid for the privilege of getting a hangover in London.

This year, with a stand ticket snug in my back pocket, I wandered around the old haunts, seeing if anything had changed. Soho was still warm and sinful, like a busty barmaid, and the streets were full of Scotsmen searching determinedly for a good time. At the door of a clip joint stood a girl wearing a mini-kilt. A large rosette was pinned to her jumper: It said: 'Scotland For Ever.' I wondered if she had a change of outfit for every occasion.

In a pub a man in a grubby raincoat came up to me and said: 'Do you want a ticket, guv?'

I looked him straight in the eye and said: 'How much?'

'Ten quid,' he said.

I leaned close and whispered a short sentence in his ear. He left hurriedly.

The incident put me in fine mood as I strode towards Wembley. Nothing has changed, I thought, as I approached the ground. Still the same tingle of excitement in the marching crowd, still the same grubby spivs selling tickets, still the same groups of fans hanging round waiting until kick-off time before putting in a bid. No, nothing's changed, I told myself. I passed a couple of lads and thought they gave me a funny look. I glanced over my shoulder and one was talking to the other and nodding in my direction. I shrugged myself deeper into my camel-hair coat, dragged nonchalantly on my cigar and wondered what they were saying. Nothing's changed, I told myself as I sank into my seat.

13

Christmas Cheer

Christmas games were special. Everything was different. Behind the goals there were more cigars than Woodbines, the bottles of Scotch flickered twixt hip and lips with the lightning speed of a humming bird's wings and the crowd rustled in its new clothes. The players were affected too, they even looked different. As a boy I imagined the change in countenance was due to the fact that they, like the rest of us, were sprinkled with Christmas stardust.

Later, as the layers of naivety slipped from me, I came to know that they were simply hungover. I first came face to face with the truth during a Christmas game some years ago when a full back on Barnsley's side played in the most erratic manner. He appeared to be unsteady on his feet and quite unable to decide which side he was on or what he was supposed to be doing. The truth dawned as he ran to take a free kick, missed the ball completely and fell flat on his back. He lay there for a while feet and arms feebly twitching until suddenly he was still and at peace.

The crowd regarded all this curiously and silently for a moment, and then someone yelled: 'Look at 'im, lying there like a roll of bloody lino.' The crowd roared and the trainer grinned sheepishly as he went to work with the smelling salts. Accounting for this unique slice of behaviour an official communiqué, issued sometime later, said that the full back had suffered an 'emotional disturbance' before the game and this had affected his play. The old man told me, on the quiet, that the emotional disturbance was caused by the change in the licensing hours at Christmas.

'Here, run after your dad. . . . He's forgotten his toilet rolls.'

To me as a child Christmas was simply a matter of how many points Barnsley took from their three games. It also meant a new pair of football boots or a shirt from a football-daft father. 'Who are you this year,' he'd ask, as I got all togged up at 5 a.m. on Christmas morning. 'George Robledo,' I'd say, and race out of doors to play a game with my imagination under the flickering gas lamps with the windows in the other houses still dark and sleeping.

In those days I became a new player every Christmas . . . George Robledo, Jackie Milburn, Peter Doherty, Stanley Matthews. And if, during the season, the player whose identity I had assumed fell from grace I would quickly transfer him to another club and pick another player. The day I stopped dreaming was the day I bought my own football boots.

The first Christmas I ever spent away from England was a melancholy one. It was difficult in Africa to make-believe Christmas in Barnsley. We did the next best thing by organising a Boxing Day football match against a team of locals. The opposion played without boots and displayed a weird assortment of skills. I was matched against a lanky and toothsome native who possessed the most staggering ball control. Time and again he dribbled the ball towards me, his toenails glinting like piano keys, and I, full of nostalgia and Army pudding, would watch his feet like a mesmerised mouse, quite unable to do anything sensible or effective.

When he'd had enough of teasing he would slip by me as if I were invisible and as he did so, just rub it in, he'd bellow 'Stanley Bloody Mathews' and laugh triumphantly. This kind of humiliation had gone on for far too long when I was approached by our left full back, a squat, hard little man from Doncaster, who was renowned for his simple and uncompromising attitude towards life and football.

'Th'art using wrong tactics against him, sir,' he said.

'Really,' I said, 'and what, pray, do you suggest?'

'He needs cloggin', sir,' the full back said.

'Cloggin'?' I queried, acting dumb.

'Pinnin', clobberin' . . . *stuffin*',' he replied.

I said I got the message. I thought the proposition over. I considered the effect that this new tactic might have on world-wide race relations and wondered further whether or not at Christmas, of all time, I ought to sanction the kind of local war the full back was suggesting. But I was too full of self-pity and misery to care. 'Go ahead. But be gentle,' I said. The full back grinned and moved away to mark the winger. The first time they met the winger showed him the ball and flicked it past him and was away with a derisive shout of 'Stanley Bloody Matthews'. I grinned pityingly at the full back, but I could have spared him my sympathy.

The next round was all his. As the winger moved down-field, the ball dancing at his feet, the full back struck like forked lightning. There was the terrible noise of bone on bone, and a flash of toenails and pink soles as the full back took the winger and the ball over the touchline. After a while the winger opened his eyes and looked dazedly and questioningly about him. The full back, standing arms folded and surveying his handiwork, stared back and answered the question. 'Wilf Bloody Copping,' he explained. It was the only whiff of home I had all that African Christmas.

The best Christmases of all were when we travelled away with Barnsley with the light ale under the seats and the kids on the luggage racks. The men, free from the pits and full of best bitter, filled the compartment with football talk and we kids, wrapped tight in new clothing, sat above them and got drunk on their arguments and their memories.

In those simple daft days nothing was more important than the coming match. We were ruled by a passion that relegated everything, no matter what, to second place. And if Barnsley won we'd speed home on silver wheels with the compartment full of bottle tops and singing. At the station someone would always ask: 'And how've you gone on?' And we'd always say: 'Two points and eight pints of bitter.' When we reached home the old woman would look at the old man as he came through the door and she'd know by his face what had happened.

If he was smiling she'd nip upstairs and get changed and they'd both go off for a Christmas drink at the boozer, leaving me at home to nurse the memories of the day like a hot-water bottle.

Today, of course, it's all changed. This Christmas I didn't see a single football match and somehow I didn't miss it. I worried about it a bit and I looked at my eldest son for signs of reassurance, for some indication that he had inherited the family's football fever.

'How did Chelsea go on today?' I asked.

'Don't know, but I tell you what, Daddy, Batman's being turned into an iced lolly.' His eyes stood out like gobstoppers.

'It's about time Tommy Docherty transferred him,' I said peevishly, and reached out for a bottle of pain-killer.

14

The Hard Mob

According to statistics compiled by one of our daily news-papers the fairest team in all the land is Nottingham Forest. They have come top of what the survey calls, in its very British way, the Fair Play League. It means that by remembering what they were taught at school about ankle-tapping and kicking people in front of the royal box Nottingham Forest have been adjudged the most sporting team in the whole of the Football League. Now this sort of gimmick normally leaves me cold. But out of sheer curiosity I looked to see where my old team, Barnsley, were placed. And before doing so I made a little bet with myself. About third from the bottom, I thought, with pride. But not so. Barnsley are adjudged to be the fourth-best behaved side in the Fourth Division and one of the most mild-mannered sides in the land.

I have not quite got over the shock. I doubt if I ever will. After twenty years of watching Barnsley I count myself an expert on the many different ways that a player can be fouled. Nothing shocks me any more, not body-checking, nor knee-hacking, nor eye-gouging, nor groin-kicking, nor the art of handing an opponent what is known locally and fondly as a 'knuckle sandwich'. I have seen it all in twenty years at Barnsley.

Furthermore, my education in these matters has been greatly enhanced by watching Barnsley play local derbies with such worthy and knowledgeable opponents as Doncaster Rovers and Rotherham United. And where are they in the Fair Play League? Rotherham, according to the statistics, are the sixth most sportsmanlike team in the Second Division, which is, from my vivid recollections, nonsense. Doncaster are only six places away from being the dirtiest team in the Third Division, which is more like it. Doncaster, it would seem, are the only team to get a fair deal from the Fair Play League. The fate of Barnsley and Rotherham serves only to stretch the cynical leer that spreads itself over my normally impassive features when anyone mentions statistics.

Only by means of statistical analysis could you alter the certain facts that the three dirtiest teams in the football league are Barnsley, Doncaster and Rotherham. The Fair Play League is asking me to erase from my mind the memories of those lovely days when it was always three o'clock in the afternoon and raining gently and the crowd wrapped itself round you smelling of tobacco and tweed like your favourite uncle. And out in the middle the Barnsley lads were getting stuck in. If the Fair Play League had been operating in those days and Barnsley had been labelled as a fair and sportsmanlike side two things might have happened. If the allegation were untrue the newspaper office could stand a very good chance of being burnt to the ground, and if, on the other hand, it were correct then the ground would be empty.

The joy in those games at Barnsley, Doncaster and Rotherham was in the sheer physical conflict between men who did not support the theory that football is a game for cream puffs. There seems now, looking back, to have been a gladiatoral attraction in those encounters. They hinged on the prowess and the durability of the hard men. With Barnsley there was Skinner Normanton, one of the best frighteners ever to grace the game, Rotherham had Wally Ardron, the bravest centre forward who ever drew breath, and Doncaster had Syd Bycroft, with the shiny

'*Top terms, a house, and the hand of the chairman's daughter in marriage.*'

slick hair and dark good looks and a tackle like a beartrap.

The games between Doncaster and Rotherham attracted thousands of people whose sole interest was to see Ardron versus Bycroft. They were magnificent and ruthless opponents. I like to think that their Maker fashioned them out of Yorkshire slag and when he had done took them on one side and said: 'Now, Walter and Syd, your job is to go on to a football field and kick lumps off one another.' And they did. They both created legends in South Yorkshire as lasting and heroic as any that hang from a gunslinger's gunbelt.

I once followed Syd Bycroft to the Doncaster bus after a game at Barnsley in which he had chipped a few edges off the local players and had been loudly abused by the home crowd throughout the game. The bus was surrounded by Barnsley fans all longing to pull Syd's hat over his eyes. But they fell apart as Bycroft walked steadily towards them. Nobody said a word until he reached the bottom step of the bus, and then someone said sarcastically: 'Enjoy thissen today, Syd?' Bycroft turned and his dark eyes flicked over the lot of us. 'Lovely,' he said, without a smile, and was gone. But even Syd Bycroft had nothing on a certain centre half who played for Barnsley just after the war. Before his home début I was standing with the old man in the paddock when a man next to us said he had watched the new centre half as a junior.

'What's he like, then?' the old man asked.

'A good 'un,' said the man.

'Where's he come from?'

'From t'pit, of course.'

'Ah, that'll be all right, then. What's he good at?' the old man enquired.

Our neighbour thought for a while and then said: 'Kickin'.'

'Kickin'?' said the old man.

'Ay, kickin'. Owt above t'grass that moves he'll kick it. He's a good 'un, this lad.'

As it turned out this was a fair description of the centre half's prowess. I once saw an international centre forward run away from him in a cup game and spend the afternoon gibbering on the wing. In later years, when I came to know the centre half, I recalled this particular incident. He remembered it well. 'I used a bit of psychology in that game,' he said proudly. I asked him what that must be. 'Well, just before t'game started I went up to this centre forward and said: "You've got a choice." And he said, "What's this choice you're talking about?" And I said, "Barnsley 'ospital or Sheffield Infirmary. Where's tha' want to go?" I never saw him again all afternoon. Didn't have to lay a finger on him.'

Faced with a set of first-hand experiences like that do you blame me that I don't believe what I read. I wish to give evidence before the Fair Play League who have already done irreparable damage to Barnsley's reputation. I shall lean heavily for support on the words attributed to a man, who, so far as I know, never stood in the paddock at Barnsley. His name was Disraeli and he once quipped. 'There are three sorts of lie: lies, damned lies and statistics.'

15

The Taller they are . . .

Serious-minded students of soccer such as myself are finding it increasingly difficult to chart the course of the modern game. No sooner do we master the new tactical innovations, such as everyone wearing everyone else's shirt, than we find ourselves face to face with some new subtlety.

The most recent development in the game was heralded by Tony Hateley and Wyn Davies, two tall centre forwards, being transferred for very large sums of money. Justifying their outlay the managers of the clubs that bought them gave a hint to soccer's next phase.

Both managers declared their firm belief that football matches in the future are going to be won in the air. They have decided that the only way to beat packed defences is to sling high crosses on to the hard head of a very tall centre forward in the hope that he will nod the ball into goal.

The simplicity of the idea is appealing, and a welcome sign that after all the technical clap-trap being talked about soccer recently some people at least have come around to the idea that it is a simple game, watched by simple people.

This latest development is, of course, of great significance to very tall centre forwards who don't mind what they do with their heads. A new life of glamour and riches is theirs for the taking.

. . . who, in the last minute, had the misfortune to put past his own 'keeper . . .' (By courtesy of Punch)

The problem here is one of genetics. We are not a very tall people. I read somewhere that the average Englishman is 5 ft. 9 in., reads the *Daily Express* and has two pairs of false teeth in his lifetime. So one can see that if the latest development in soccer is to come to pass then football managers will have to look elsewhere for their material.

This is where tall people, like the Tutsi of Rwanda and Burundi and Ona of Tierra del Fuego, Chile, come into their own. The giant men of these tribes should stop whatever they are doing and start learning to head a football.

Scene: An encampment of the Tutsi, a proud and tall warrior race. Sixteen football managers from England sit in an improvised stand, their pockets stuffed with cheap trinkets and book tokens. On a rough-and-ready patch hacked out of the bush Tutsi Albion are playing Tutsi Dynamo (using turbans for goalposts). The centre of attraction is Lionel N'gooda, the dynamic centre forward of Tutsi Albion.

Lionel stands 8 ft. 9 in. in his cheap plastic football boots made in Hong Kong. He scores twelve goals in the game, all with his head, and afterwards is surrounded by football managers fighting for his services. Eventually he is sold to Chelsea for eight tubes of wine gums, two cases of cheap Australian sherry and three plastic raincoats.

In England Lionel is an immediate success. Desmond Dribbel calls him 'Leaping Lionel', and says of him: 'N'gooda is V'gooda. A black panther, a dusky sensation.'

Lionel scores seventy-two goals in his first season with Chelsea, all with his head. Soon he opens his first boutique called, 'I'm High Daddy. Clothes for the taller man.' He is frequently seen in the company of Tommy Docherty. The canny Scot says: 'Lionel speaks very good English.' He is even more frequently seen with Lady Daphne Kippington-Bedsprings, London's tallest deb, who says: 'I always felt out of it until I met Lionel.'

Like all successful people Lionel makes enemies. A group of soccer managers, meeting secretly, decide that the only way to combat this growing menace of tall centre forwards is to find even taller centre halves. They employ the brilliant but evil talents of Professor J. Achestein-Fink.

In his laboratory in Zürich the Professor, the man who developed the jumbo drug for shot-putters and the 'Anything-you-can-do' pill for women hammer-throwers, works on a new invention to beat the menace of Leaping Lionel.

After six months he develops a drug to stretch the legs and harden the head. He experiments on a 5 ft. 6 in. centre half who once played for Chesterfield. The experiment is completely successful. The centre half grows to nine foot two inches, can head guided missiles and is transferred to Tottenham Hotspur for £120,000.

In his first game against Lionel he so dominates him that the Tutsi pulls a knife and is sent from the field. Soon every First Division club in England has one of Professor Achestein-Fink's centre halves, and the Professor is able to buy Noël Coward's house in Bermuda and retire.

Lionel is unable to score any more goals and Tommy Docherty twice sends him back to his digs because he has not cleaned his teeth. Lionel eventually sells his boutique and returns to his native village where he finds his relatives have eaten his transfer fee.

In the meantime Bob Lord, Britain's caped crusader, protests to F.I.F.A. about what he calls 'these disgusting trends in our great national game'. Mr. Lord bans from his ground any player standing more than 6 ft. 3 in., saying: 'It's not natural.'

The Minister for Sport intervenes and makes a plea for 'Normalcy'. Swift action follows. The F.A. bans from the game any man standing more than 6 ft. 3 in. Bob Lord says, 'It's a triumph for Northern common sense.' The eighteen giant centre halves in the First Division are given free transfers and are hired by an American football promoter to play exhibition matches against a team of Pygmies.

Desmond Dribbel sums up. In a no-punches-pulled editorial headed 'This Sorry Mess' he concludes: 'It proves what I said at the beginning of this sad and sorry affair: the taller they are, the harder they fall.'

The Man in the Middle

'He kicked me so I bit his ear off.'
Referee giving evidence to F.A. Disciplinary Committee

16

The Unloved Ones

In the ever-changing game of soccer the lot of the referee remains the same. It is not a happy one. I have always felt sorry for referees, because the job they are expected to carry out is basically impossible.

It they are to do their work properly they have to be able to keep close to the ball throughout the ninety minutes of play, a task calling for colossal stamina. At the same time they are expected to make crucial and often very difficult decisions after chasing 100 yards in even time. Those of you who have run 100 yards in ten seconds, only to be met at the tape by a man from N.O.P. who wants to know what you think about the Common Market, will understand what I mean.

Moreover, the referee has also to contend with the baying of a hostile crowd, the tantrums and snide remarks of the players. And all this for a few bob. Referees know they are not loved except by those nearest and dearest to them. I once saw a referee at Barnsley knocked out by a heavy muddy ball, and as he lay, still and forlorn on the ground and the trainer ran across the pitch towards him, someone shouted, 'Don't revive him, bury the sod.' The rest of the crowd agreed.

The position of the referee in the modern game is probably worse than it has ever been. It is the classic example of responsibility without power. They are continually exhorted to get tougher with the players, and yet when they send off a persistent offender they know that the stiffest sentence the player will receive is a piffling £100 fine and a measly twenty-eight-day suspension.

But whatever happens to improve the lot of the referee, nothing will change his place in society. He will always be unloved by the majority of the population, and will inevitably find it necessary to walk through places like Liverpool with his collar up and his hat brim down, for fear of being recognised. The referee will always occupy that unenviable position of being one who dispenses justice and yet expects none in return.

The saddest example of the referee's plight that I know happened some time ago. His name was Ron and he worked in an office, which fact did not endear him to the majority of players he was expected to control every Saturday afternoon. Where I lived anyone with a white-collar job was a bit suspect.

Ron was the referee one day in a local Derby game between our village and a team two miles down the road. This was a fixture in which traditionally there was a lot of bloodletting. Rivalries were fierce and a few punch-ups were an accepted part of the event. The two main protagonists were our full back called Blackie and their right winger called Charlie Onions.

Charlie Onions was completely bald and shy about it, so he used to play in a flat cap. The only time he removed his cap, was on the odd occasion when he headed a ball and the more frequent occasions when he was involved in a punch-up. During a fight Charlie's cap became a fearsome weapon. He would fold it so that only the peak showed and then use it to belabour his opponent. The moments when Charlie removed his cap in anger were eagerly awaited by his supporters, who would encourage him with cries of 'Gi' him some bloody neb, Charlie'.

Blackie, on the other hand, was quieter, but just as deadly. He was one of those footballers who never said a

'*Oh come, chaps . . . I wasn't all that good!*' (By courtesy of *Punch*)

word, never squealed if you fouled him, but simply awaited the opportunity to get his own back. Always his revenge was swift and terrible. His battles with Charlie Onions were legendary and eagerly anticipated by the crowd.

On the day of the match, Ron, the referee, made it obvious that, tradition or not, he wasn't going to have any monkey business. He warned both Charlie and Blackie that if they started anything he'd send them off.

The game was only five minutes old when Charlie Onions took his cap off to Blackie. Immediately the referee intervened and warned both of them that the next time it happened they would be sent off.

Five minutes later and Charlie again had his cap off to Blackie after a tackle which nearly parted him from his ankles.

The referee raced up to them.

'Off, off,' he shouted.

The two players looked at one another. 'Nay, ref, we're only just warmin' up,' said Charlie.

'Off, off,' said the ref, who was getting very excited.

Blackie said: 'Na' look, ref, me and Charlie don't mean 'owt when we start fightin' and it's what t'crowd expects. So why don't tha' leave us alone?'

The ref was nearly beside himself with frustration and rage. 'Off, off or else I abandon the game,' he shouted.

Blackie looked at Charlie Onions and said, 'Tha' knows, Charlie, I've played this game fifteen years and nivver been sent off, and I've allus said when I do get t'marching orders it will be for summat special. Na', old mate, I don't regard cloggin' thee as being owt special, does tha'?' Charlie shook his head. 'Therefore,' said Blackie, 'I'm about to mek a proper job of things.' Whereupon he turned to the referee and felled him with a colossal right swing.

'Tha's done right,' said Charlie, as he walked off the field with Blackie.

Two weeks later Blackie was in the boozer when they brought the news. Len, the trainer, said to him, 'They've banned thi' *sine die*.'

'Is that bad?' asked Blackie.

'It means for good, that's all,' said Len.

'That's all right then. I wor ready for retirin', any road,' said Blackie.

Blackie didn't suffer. Later that season they held a benefit game for him. The posters advertising the game said, 'Proceeds for a deserving charity', because they couldn't announce they were collecting for a banned player. The referee, on the other hand, got little sympathy from anyone, and eventually went to live in Wakefield.

If you go back to the village now they'll still point Blackie out to you, and tell you how he fixed the referee.

All he did was to express in one massive right-arm swing what anyone who has ever been to a football match has felt at one time or another. We've all nurtured a secret desire to chin the referee. Knowing this, and knowing also that the referee is aware of it too, I am filled with wonderment and amazement every time I see them trot on to the field of play. How many men do you know who would walk into the jaws of Hell knowing that their only reward is a few bob and the scorn of their fellow men?

Sex and Sport

'If you had played football none of this would have happened.'
Magistrate sending eighteen-year-old labourer to three months'
imprisonment for non-payment of maintenance order

17

A Cautionary Tale

The idea that sport and sex do not mix is firmly implanted in British thinking. We further believe that sport is the antidote to sex, that evil thoughts about girlies are banished by a brisk game of table tennis, followed by a cold shower. It is my theory that we achieved our reputation as a nation of sports lovers not because we are particularly fond of sport but because we are appallingly shy about sex.

In other words, the playing fields of England are full of young people, not because their parents are desperately keen for them to learn the skills of football, but because they hope to delay the awful day when their boy discovers that girls are deliciously different from himself.

We have clung to this belief when all the evidence points in the opposite direction and only serves to show that the playing fields of England are training grounds for the bed-chamber. Women adore sportsmen and any youth who is packed off by his parents in search of healthy and innocent sport on the playing field is, in truth, being launched on a collision course towards members of the opposite sex.

This theory of mine that sex and sport do mix (nay, I'll go further and state that one leads to the other) has now been accepted by the Football League. In its magazine this august organisation has recently been encouraging girls to name the sexiest footballers in the land. At present the top pin-ups are Georgie Best of Manchester United, Gerry Bridgwood of Stoke, and Rodney Marsh of Q.P.R.

This daring piece of journalism, which breaks down the old taboos, delights me as it must those thousands of enlightened parents who have been worrying about how to unload the facts of life on to their children. All they have to do now is buy him a pair of football boots and leave the rest to nature.

But before they do I have a cautionary tale to tell involving sex and Squat White. Squat was the inside right in a team I used to play with, a good footballer but strikingly unbeautiful. He was in fact the first captain of my first World Ugly XI. The team we played for was called the Congs, an abbreviation of the Congregational Chapel. None of us actually attended the Chapel, except our captain, who ran the team in the fond belief that football was spiritually uplifting and that we would all benefit by kicking lumps off one another every Saturday afternoon.

He received his first lesson in disenchantment the day we played a cup game at a nearby pit village. Our opponents included five brothers who formed a defence which kept the local outpatients department in regular employment. We were changing under a railway bridge near the ground (which made a pleasant change from stripping in the hedge bottom as was normal) when the five brothers appeared.

'Which one is it, then?' asked the biggest one.

'I beg your pardon,' said our captain.

'Which one of your lot got our Gladys in trouble, then?' asked another brother.

Our captain went pale with rage. How dare these monsters suggest that one of his team would dally with their Gladys. Didn't they know that football kept a young man free from such evil thoughts. He had just started saying as much when the biggest brother interrupted.

'Don't deny it. Tha's only got to look at our Gladys to

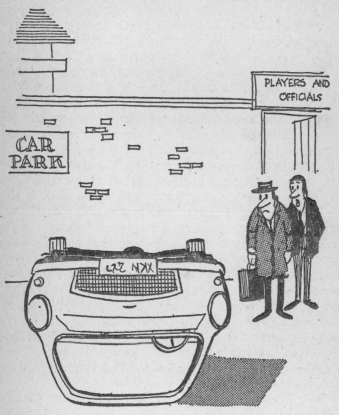

"You know what baffles me, ref? . . . How did they know it was yours?"

see what happened. She's in trouble and she says that it wor a Cong that did it. She won't gi' us his name but we're going to find out and when we do then he's got a choice.'

'What's that?' said the captain.

'Church or t'Infirmary,' said the big brother, glaring at the lot of us.

They left us saying they would give us until the start of the game to name the culprit. Our skipper looked around. 'Who's been playing silly buggers, then?' he said.

Slowly Squat White raised his hand. At first we didn't believe him. He was the last person you would expect anyone called Gladys to fall for. But he finally convinced us with a graphic description of how Gladys had accosted him after one game, told him he looked like Peter Doherty and asked him to accompany her on a blackberrying expedition.

'Will I have to wed her?' said Squat.

'Does tha' want to?' asked the skipper.

Squat shook his head. 'But I don't want to end up in t'Infirmary either,' he said.

'Well, we'll just have to tell 'em that they've made a mistake, that their Gladys got mixed up in t'teams,' said the skipper.

The brothers greeted this news contemptuously. The biggest one said: 'We'll just have to clog t'lot of you to mek sure that t'culprit doesn't escape.' His brothers nodded in agreement and seemed delighted at the prospect ahead. There were times during the ensuing ninety minutes when all of us felt like squealing on Squat, if only to stop the kicking, gouging and hacking But we battled silently on and finished losing 5—0 with six men still standing.

At the final whistle the biggest brother said: 'We'll be coming for you when we've got changed and we'll have t'old man wi' us and some of his mates to sort you lot out proper.'

We fled to our bridge, grabbed our clothes and, without bothering to change, ran fearfully to the bus-stop carrying our wounded. On the bus our skipper said to Squat, 'Tha's disappointed me, Squat. Tha' sees now wheer all this petticoat-huntin' leads thi'.'

Squat nodded miserably.

A few weeks later Gladys shopped Squat to her brothers and they came looking for him. Being a sensible lad, he decided on marriage, rather than an unspecified time in the Infirmary, and left our club to join his brothers-in-law.

The real casualty in the affair was our skipper, who was cruelly shown that far from sport being an antidote to sex that he believed it was in fact an aphrodisiac. He gave up football and bought some racing pigeons. I regarded what had happened as a useful experience, one that enabled me to give sport its proper place in the rich tapestry of life.

For instance, when I bought my eldest son his first pair of football boots I knew exactly what I was doing. Not keeping him out of trouble but equipping him for the first round of the battle of the sexes.